FREE THE
CBI

Power Games in Bhopal & other Cases

Attention Authors

Manas Publications is fighting a war to tell the world that India can win the battle not only by the bullet but also by pen. We are converting fighters into writers. There is no dearth of intellectuals in our country, however, their knowledge is confined to them only. No sincere effort has been made by any other publisher to channelise their knowledge, that is why the talent of every intellectual remains latent. An author always presents the raw material in the shape of a manuscript and it is the job of the publisher to convert it to a finished product. Manas has been continually motivating intellectuals and publishing their manuscripts for more than two decades and would like to publish your manuscript too. If you or your colleagues have a manuscript ready for publication or are working on it, contact us with a detailed synopsis and list of contents. Manas can also suggest you a suitable title for writing related to your area of expertise. Manas is known for its publishing quality. We take utmost care in publishing and also give wide publicity to the book and its author through our national and international distribution network.

FREE THE
CBI

Power Games in Bhopal & other Cases

BR Lall, IPS (Retd)
Former: Joint Director, CBI
DGP – Haryana

Manas Publications
(We Convert Fighters into Writers)
New Delhi-110002 (INDIA)

MANAS PUBLICATIONS
(Publishers, Library Suppliers, Importers & Exporters)
4402/5-A, Ansari Road (Opp. HDFC Bank)
Darya Ganj, New Delhi-110 002 (INDIA)
Off. ✆ 23260783, 23265523, Res. ✆ 23842660
Fax: 011-23272766
E-mail: manaspublications@vsnl.com
manaspublications@yahoo.com

ISBN 978-81-7049-396-9
₹ 495

Typeset at
Manas Publications

Printed in India at
RK Print Services, Delhi
and published by Mrs Suman Lata for
Manas Publications, 4402/5-A, Ansari Road
(Opp. HDFC Bank),
Darya Ganj, New Delhi-110 002 (INDIA)

Contents

Preface

The situation arising out of the Bhopal Gas case, the worst industrial tragedy that the world ever faced, was highly mismanaged not only by the UCC (Union Carbide Corporation) but also by the Central Government, the state government, as also the judiciary. The position taken by the UCC is understandable as right from the beginning they did not want to own any responsibility, which is normal for any business undertaking unless it faces the heat from the law. However, the stance taken by the Government of India from time to time is beyond comprehension, that too after it assumed the responsibility for fighting the case on behalf of all the victims, but abandoning them high and dry in all respects, including compromising the virtual genocide of 5000–15000 people, by entering into the devastating pact with UCC and above all agreeing to waive the criminal liability. The courts took 23 years in, practically, scuttling the case. For a change, it is only the most maligned CBI that stood firm in investigating the case fully and firmly withstanding all the pressures, though its role also comes under the scanner for not filing review petition in the Supreme Court after the 1996 judgment that took away all the punch from the case and downgraded the worst industrial tragedy to the level of an ordinary motor vehicle accident. Of course, the CBI has to seek permission from the Government for filing such a review, but it is to be seen whether it was a decision of the Government or the CBI buckled down under pressure and compromised its conscience like all other agencies of the state, after all continuous pressures do blunt the conscience. The trail of the pressures continued even in the aftermath of the June 2010 decision of the Lower Court. This book is a humble attempt to lay bare before the nation the entire process of errors and pressures in the right perspective by the author who has been an insider and watched the Government as also the CBI from very close angles.

BR Lall

brlall@gmail.com

Introduction

On the afternoon of 7th June 2010 my telephone rang to inform me about the judgment in the Bhopal Gas Tragedy case. The voice at the other end identified itself as someone from the media. I expressed my surprise why he was informing me. Since I was in a conference at Delhi, I switched off my mobile. In the evening the moment I switched it on during my journey back home to Gurgaon, I got a number of calls from media enquiring about the arrest of the then UCC (Union Carbide Corporation) chief, Warren Anderson, his release on the same day, i.e. 7th December 1984 and the later pressures not to pursue his extradition case in the context of the Bhopal Gas Tragedy. Though I was surprised how all of a sudden they were swooping on me, but I am not a person to hesitate from speaking out the truth bluntly at any time or on any occasion. I informed that I was not concerned either with his arrest or with release, but confirmed that during my posting in CBI from 26th April 1994 to July 1995 I supervised the Bhopal Gas Tragedy case, as one of the branches under my charge was handling it and that we had received a communication that had originated in the Ministry of External Affairs (MEA), that desired us (the CBI) not to pursue the extradition case of Warren Anderson. We had written back that he was the prime accused and that he could not be spared as we required him in the case very badly. We opposed the orders of MEA and continued to pursue the case vigorously in the court. I had specially summoned the prosecutor handling this case from Bhopal, discussed the matter in details, briefed and strengthened him to pursue the case with utmost vigour and tenacity.

By the time I reached home at Gurgaon it was rather late. Early in the morning of the next day, the 8th of June, people from the TV channels and the print media started pouring in at my residence, unannounced. My interviews with media commenced in the morning and as they started airing, a prompt outburst came from the Law Minister Moily reacting violently. I was surrounded by the media persons and could not watch his reaction myself, but I became aware as the subsequent interviewers started questioning me on that too. That very night I got a mail from a UK based journalist, (who had watched the violent reaction of the Law Minister Moily), apologizing for all the muck that was being created. He felt apologetic that he had landed me in trouble. Operative part of his mail is reproduced below.

"I am sorry that you are being subject to personal attacks by India's corrupt elite. If there is any good to come of what may be becoming personal ordeal, it is that a governmental enquiry be initiated into the circumstances of India's capitulation to political influences from the US."

He also informed me of having posted the following on *The Times of India* web site "The outrageous slur on BR Lall's character by two Government ministers demonstrates the truth of his testimony. Mr Khurshid accuses Mr Lall of trying to become a media icon. I can testify that Mr Lall did nothing at all to break the story. I personally spoke with him two weeks ago about his book *Who Owns CBI: The Naked Truth* and during the conversation Mr Lall disclosed the story of MEA's interference with due process in the Bhopal prosecution. Mr Lall represents a class of public servants that in my small experience, is reassuringly present in many parts of India's bureaucracy, but remains generally unheralded, undervalued and obscured by the prominence of a minority of venal self serving individuals. Mr Lall is the precise opposite of a glory seeker and he is a principled and fearless truth teller."

That connected why media were swooping on me. He had placed our conversation that took place some weeks back, over the Internet. Incidentally, since 1995 I had been mentioning this story in the drawing rooms and other social and general conversations and regretting that government of India had done wrong in negotiating Indian lives and that too for peanuts, i.e. for a measly sum of $ 470 million (including 80 millions of interest component since December 1984), though our claims pending in the court were as high as $ 3.3 billion. There was no ostensible reason to settle for just the 14% of our claim and more so to dilute criminal liability in the case that was altogether a separate issue. Although the criminal liability was subsequently restored by the time I came to the scene to handle the case in CBI in 1994, but the original agreement did weaken our case and when I chanced to see the papers from USA that some of my contacts have sent, these are replete with the recurring strain that in February 1989, the settlement freed everyone from the criminal liability, so no criminal case could stand in Indian courts and the civil part could not be an issue at all after the settlement. The Bhopal issue was a closed chapter as per the perception of the people in USA. The missive from the MEA that I had spoken about is a logical fallout of the same agreement and the mindset that prevailed in the MEA at Delhi as well and has to be realistically viewed and appreciated in that light and everything then falls into place consistently. At that time, it was in view of the bilateral relations, that the Government might have seen some merit that they could reiterate and clarify, but now the line they adopted is of pure denial by the mighty ministers, for reasons best known to them, though pitted against the glaring truth, their bluff tumbled out in the next few days. In the process, the so-called honourable people turned into and behaved like *Dadas* and mafia dons trying to muzzle the truth and throttle the voice that spoke truth, that they perceived was against them. There were also a few angry exchanges between them and me over the TV channels, both live and recorded, though some of the channels resorted to heavy editing in the recorded versions, of the simple facts that I had put forth.

Before long Moti Singh, the District Magistrate (DM) of Bhopal in 1984, came on the air and corroborated about the pressures as I had said. Then the party men from the ruling Congress started making statements against each other, every person defending his own role and in the process Arjun Singh as also the Government of India at that time came under a cloud. Digvijay Singh who was travelling abroad laid the responsibility at the doors of the then Union Government. The controversies and hitting the ball into the court of all others continued, but one thing good that has come out is that all this and the resultant public mood swing has compelled the attention of the Government to be focussed on the medication and rehabilitation of the victims as also the clearing of the toxic waste that still threatens the lives of the people of Bhopal and the ecology of the town. Now, in retrospect, I feel grateful to the journalist to whom I had narrated the facts in routine *gap-shap,* but he, it appears, per chance focussed them for the good of the people. But for him, I must confess I would not have come out of the drawing room conversation.

Another issue that cropped up during this media turmoil requiring greater attention is on the various pressures, and the build-up on all the investigating agencies in the country including the CBI, that does not permit them to perform their sacrosanct statutory functions of collection of facts objectively without any bias, fear or favour. People witnessed first-hand, that what to speak of talking truth while in service, it is not tolerated even from the retired personnel. By God's grace, it is a different matter that nobody, even the highest, could ever pressurise me during my 37 years of service as an IPS officer and by God's grace, I was fortunate to stand up against the illegal orders even from the Prime Minister and opposed the same successfully and was not cowed down even when it meant going against the ruling Prime Minister himself. In the process during my service I was transferred a number of times, tossed around, but these are minor matters. I feel satisfied that in my own humble way, I kept the torch of integrity and truth burning, though I must confess that every time it was transfer from the then crucial position and that I could not finish the task. In CBI it happened in the Jain Hawala case, in cases of V Krishnamurthy, the Assam LOC scandal involving Hiteshwar Saikia, the then CM of Assam, besides a number of cases in my state cadre. Desperate at the manner in which I was shifted in CBI from that zone, so that these cases and in particular the Jain Hawala case could be scuttled, I published an article in the *Hindustan Times* of 1st March 1996 titled *How to Make CBI a Free Agency* (copy attached as Appendix – I) as otherwise it could not act against the big people. Later even the CVC has not been found adequate to measure up with the immense problem of fighting corruption at high places and against the higher ups. However, a moving first-hand account, illustrated with the actual correspondence, of the pressures in these cases could be interesting and educative for the people who wonder how and why even the honest public servants, generally keeping themselves personally clean, do not act according to the dictates of law and facts, and submit to the pressures against their will and their conscience.

I propose to take up the Bhopal issue as I was concerned with it and how has it been viewed when it unfolded itself and later I propose to move to my experiences about the pressures exerted in particular on CBI and on the state police in general in the field of investigations and how difficult it is to fight them, but at the same time to show that one can stand-up against all this mafia like build-up, though the risks involved are tremendous. The resistance to pressures may not produce immediate results but does make some invisible impact as they say that if head is hit against the mighty Himalayas, it may break but at the same time mathematically, even the great mountains move though imperceptibly and infinitesimally. The struggle needs to be continued and this book is a small step in that direction and to clear up the misconceptions created in the process.

Appendix – I

How to Make CBI a Free Agency

BR Lall

JACOB G. Grossberg, deposing before the commission on graft and organised crime in 1933 in the US, said: "Politics is the business of the party organisation, party organisation is the business of the mercenary criminal, the racketeer. The political boss is usually the well-paid agent or manager for the latter, and the men he puts in office are usually puppets... the policeman on the beat or the plainclothes man does not bring in the big shot, whose gang controls his ward committee chief, who controls his captain, who controls him. It is the party organisation which furnishes the Governor, the Judge, the Prosecutor, and which gives orders to the police. In other words, it furnishes the law enforcing organisation. It is manifest that that organism suffers paralysis...and a paralysed body cannot function properly."

In place of the word 'police' in the above quote, we can read administration in its entirety. It is the administration in totality which is suffering from paralysis.

In this country we have specialised agencies in all the states and the Central Bureau of Investigation (CBI) at the Centre. We must understand its dynamics before the crucial questions are answered. Corruption is a game and prerogative of people in power. Basically corruption is nothing but conversion of power (both political and administrative) into money. The anti-corruption organisation to be effective should be capable of taking action against persons in power but the bureaucratic functioning including these agencies suited the times of British rule where it was a master-servant relationship. The slave cannot question the actions of the master or disobey his orders.

Even an upright official, when faced with orders from his political masters, turn helpless in an effort to uphold rules and values. He is seen to be disloyal as if loyalty is not to the system but to the individual. Even wise people have become players in this sordid drama. The investigative agencies do real good work, otherwise, but when it comes to exposing a person in high office, be he a political master, or a bureaucrat, they shake and tremble. They are used to functioning under the political masters' directions only.

The rules and procedures under which the registration, the investigation, the enquiry or verification of criminal misconduct are to be initiated against the high and mighty, dissuade the agency and stonewall all the legal processes. The safeguards enjoyed by these persons offer near-immunity from any action by these agencies against those in power. This applies to the highest agency of the land, the CBI. It is a well-known fact that the CBI has to seek the permission of the Government for every step it takes.

Persons in power who indulge in corruption can be expected to make every effort to block the investigation even if some cases have to be taken up as a result of a public outcry. Investigating officers who function under these very masters keep weighing the political fallout and consequences.

There are executive instructions overriding the laws of the land to seek permission for making enquiries, for registering criminal cases, for conducting searches, in case of persons beyond a certain level in office which reminds one of that strict warden who prescribed: "Nobody will move out of the hostel without my permission and be sure that permission will not be granted."

The job of the agency is to find and collect facts in the most truthful manner without any consideration other than the law and without any fear, favour or pressure. The CBI or any other authority that may be created needs to be placed under a board of control. The job of the Government is to maintain law and order which is not the job of the CBI. If taken out of the Government's control, the normal functions of the Government will not be affected in any way except that corrupt public servants will not be able to indulge fearlessly into this all degrading nefarious activity.

The mechanism of appointment of the CBI control board (or whatever other name we may give to this autonomous high-powered body) should not be dependent upon any recommendations or a selection process. The members of the board should come up in their own right rather than being appointed and be beholden to anyone. The board should be headed by a retired Chief Justice or a judge of the Supreme Court and include a retired Comptroller and Auditor General of India (CAG) and a former Director, CBI as members with the serving Director/CBI as its non-participating secretary. The term of each members and the Chairman shall be for two years. The Chairman shall have the same status, perks and salary as that of Chief Justice/Judge of the Supreme Court and the other two equivalent to that of the Comptroller and Auditor General of India. They should be removable only through the process of impeachment as provided for judges and the CAG.

The board will exercise all the operational functions of the Government in the context of all the CBI cases against corruption. The CBI board should be treated as appointing authority for all the suspects against whom the agency proceeds or proposes commencement of enquiries, investigations, and grant of permission for prosecution under the PC Act. The Government will cease to have any operational control over CBI. Since the position of DCBI will become very crucial, his appointment will also vest in the board and it will be a term posting. The rules governing him will have to be worked out in detail, but in brief, his term could be three years like the chief of a defence force. An IPS officer with a very good track record and having put in at least 30 years of service should be eligible. The Government of India could sponsor five to seven names but there will be no bar on considering other names by the board.

The board members and the DCBI shall be prohibited from undertaking any job under any Government or Private Sector, barred from following any business or profession after a term on the board and also there shall be no extension as a member of the board or DCBI under any circumstance. The status of the DCBI should be raised to that of service chiefs.

The above will free the chief investigating agency from undesirable extraneous controls and also from the allegations that it follows the dictates of political masters or that it acts to serve their political ends. It will restore the confidence of the people. The prospect of action against the high and mighty is going to deter and prevent the high-ups from indulging in unlawful activities.

(Mr BR Lall is a serving, senior IPS officer)

Chapter - I

Bhopal Gas Tragedy: A Chronological Account

It is well known that the tragedy occurred on the night intervening 2nd and 3rd December, 1984 and the FIR was registered by the Bhopal police on the morning of 3rd under Section 304 A of IPC, for rash and negligence act. At that time there was complete confusion and nobody had any inkling as to what had exactly happened, much less the reasons for the same. The first information was registered on the initiative of the area SHO of Bhopal police suo motto as there was none to lodge a complaint. Whatever information he could gather in that confusion was reduced into the FIR against the five members of the supervisory staff on duty as per the records of the factory, giving out that the gas had leaked from the factory and that was causing the devastation. Leak was presumed to be due to negligence of workers/supervisors of Union Carbide and accordingly a case of rash and negligence act was registered. At that stage no more facts were known, nor was there any idea of the potential of the damage that the leak would cause. Besides there was no idea whose fault exactly it was. Even otherwise, a bona fide FIR lodged promptly after the event can never present a complete or a comprehensive account of the events which has to be found out during the investigations. The FIR only provides a starting point for the investigation that is supposed to throw up all the facts. In between when there is enough evidence or at the conclusion of the investigations if the evidence points to something different, the sections of law are added or deleted accordingly as the evidence may demand. Ultimately a final report is laid before the court on completion of investigations. The final report may end in chargesheet, either complete or partial or may propose closure of the case or its cancellation if the case turns out to be false.

In the process of investigation arrests, searches and all such aids/requirements are followed under the departmental supervision and the final watchful eye of the court. In this case the local police took up the investigations but the process was naturally slow as the first thing was to prevent the leakage of gas causing further damage, then to look after the ailing and the deceased. However for satisfaction of the public the five persons named in the FIR were arrested in order to join them in investigations. Till the morning of December 7, 1984 when Warren Anderson descended on Bhopal duly escorted by VIPs, the investigation had not made any progress, so the offence had not been changed to a serious one. Perhaps no more names were added to the list of accused persons. As such no names from local management or from the UCC including that of Warren Anderson appeared in the list. He, along with Keshub Mahindra and others was arrested under 304 of IPC. Basically it appears that the police were not ready to effect any further arrest as yet, so in all probability the decision to arrest Anderson was sudden and not a well considered professional one after collection of evidence by the police officers investigating it. Keshub Mahindra and others had to be arrested as otherwise the arrest of Anderson would appear misplaced by itself, as the line has first to reach the local management before being extended to the UCC in USA. The arrest appears to be under the orders of the CM as otherwise SP or DM were neither prepared operationally nor would have dared to touch a foreign dignitary, and much less a person of the stature of Anderson. Our administrators and police officers are not so daring even in case of Indian biggies despite existence of massive evidence against them. There was some speculation in the media that the CM might have decided to arrest him targeting the votes in the forthcoming parliamentary elections towards the end of December 1984. However, Anderson had to be released in the afternoon and escorted by the DM and the SP, as a VIP to the airport. The CM placed his personal plane at the disposal of Anderson. This is a rare gesture as the CMs all over the country are too reluctant to share their aircraft, which is treated more as a personal perquisite attached exclusively to them rather than the government transport that could be indented by others in the government, who may need the same for more effective discharge of their duties. Why the CM had to change his orders of arrest of Anderson and allow bail, will be examined a little later. However Bhopal was under the state of severe shock and high anxiety to take note of this technicality at that time.

The case was taken over by the CBI from the local police on the ground on 9th December and they adopted the same FIR as was filed by the local police. The CBI conducted the investigations with a high degree of professionalism and sought advice and opinion of the experts from the CSIR (Council of Scientific and Industrial Research)—a very specialised expert body on all scientific matters. Under Dr Vardarajan, the DG CSIR, the team intensively looked into all the possible technical and scientific details from all the angles and produced a comprehensive report. The CBI armed itself very well with all this evidence and fortified the same with the records of the UCIL. The CBI filed a chargesheet in the Session's Court on 01.12.1987 under Section 304 Part II IPC for culpable homicide not amounting to murder (in place of the original section of registration of offence, i.e. 304A IPC dealing with rash and negligence act) against 12 accused persons with the list being headed by the UCC Chairman Warren Anderson. The CBI had started investigating the case under Section 304A for rash and negligence act but during investigations it came to the conclusion that it was a case of culpable homicide not amounting to murder and filed the chargesheet accordingly as is clear from the following excerpts from the operative part of the chargesheet:

"The scientific team headed by Dr Vardarajan has concluded that the factors which led to the toxic gas leakage causing heavy toll included...insufficient caution in design, in choice of material for construction and in provision of measuring and alarm instruments, together with the inadequate controls on system of storage and on quality of stored materials as well as lack of necessary facilities for quick effective disposal of material exhibiting instability, led to the accident.... The evidence collected during investigation proves that the accused persons had the knowledge that by the various acts of commission and omission in the design and running of MIC plant, death and injury of various degrees could be caused to a large number of human beings and animals. All the accused persons joined in such acts of omission and commission with such common knowledge. This resulted in the incident on the night of 2nd/3rd December 1984."

Immediately after the tragedy, some attorneys in USA became active and filed legal suits in the US courts for damages/compensation totalling $15 bn and more were rushing through. However the Union Government restrained them by rushing in promulgation of an ordinance namely "Bhopal Gas Leak Disaster (Processing of claims) Ordinance 1985" on 20th February 1985. The same was enacted into a law by converting the ordinance into an Act of the Parliament on 29.3.1985. The state took over all the responsibility to fight all the suits on behalf of the citizens. It was thought to be a good step and much was made to be expected of it, but unfortunately it became a tool of collective organised surrender of Indian interests instead of protecting the same. The surrender formula was evolved in 1988-89, to which the Union Government became a signatory. It made the Act itself suspect to have been enacted under pressure from the US.

The Union of India filed a consolidated claim amounting to $3.3 bn in India for damages and compensation. This was besides the criminal case that was under investigation with CBI and latter on under trial in the court.

In February 1989 a settlement was reached between the Government of India and the Union Carbide, settling all the outstanding matters both civil and criminal for a compensation of $470 million. The UCC had originally offered to pay $350 million plus interest that added up to $426 million, whereas after scaling down the demand from $3300 million, the negotiators of the Government of India were stuck at only $500 million. Both the sides left it to the Supreme Court that moderated the amount in between at $470 million. This was a sell out as cases worth $15 bn duly filed in courts were withdrawn post haste and a revised claim of $3.3 bn was filed. The agreement however reduced it further drastically. Bargains do take place and there is always give and take at the margins even in the serious matters, but in this most serious case there was no marginal adjustment but surrender of 86% of the already reduced demand, settling at just as 14% of the original projections of the Government. After all, initially also the damages and compensation must have been worked out for some numbers and on the basis of some criterion and that all would have been changed post haste while accepting 14% of the claim, otherwise how could the original projections be ignored accepting just a peanut that is 1/7th of our original demand filed in the court in India and just the 3% of what had been filed in the USA as early as 20th February 1985. It is correct that the attorneys there would have retained a handsome chunk, but even if a half or even a one-third of the amount was given to the victims, that would have been manifold as compared to the amount settled. Incidentally, many more cases were on way to the US courts when the law came in between as a great relief to the UCC.

Besides the above sell out of the claims, the criminal liability which was something altogether different, was also sacrificed at the altar of this measly compensation. We must have looked foolish to ourselves and the world would have laughed at our capacity to bend down or get blackmailed under the pressures, sacrificing all the self interest. Self interest is the cornerstone of all the diplomacy of any sovereign nation. Under no circumstances and for any compensation, can a self respecting country bargain for criminal liability in such a serious case, whereas we bargained it and that too with a heavy surrender of our claims. There was no compulsion to settle for such a low amount and the bargain literally drowned the victims in 1989 itself. Supposing for a minute, if at all this was to be done, 2-3 issues were required to be straightened beforehand. First, even a naive will appreciate that if criminal liability was also to be settled, the compensation should have rocketed up from our original claims, adding penalty/punishment for the criminal act but actually it went down that too steeply. Secondly, such a factory with all its assets should automatically have lapsed to the government, without any compensation, so there could not be any question of sale of its shares that should have remained impounded. Third, the area was to be cleansed of toxic materials as otherwise it was capable of spreading further contamination. Immense resources and technical know-how were required that were available with the UCC as it is their area of expertise. The agreement should have asked them to cleanse it, that too within a given time frame. Incidentally that is an issue hanging fire till this day, as it has now come to public domain that till today such risks loom large over the township. It is not in hindsight, but was the prevailing public sentiment at that time and in 1994-95 when I saw the case files in CBI, this impression was very clearly reflected. The Supreme Court also erred in throwing out the case including the criminal liability, in 1989. If the Government had blundered, the Supreme Court should have come to the rescue of the people and not approved and much less not mediated the deal, but alas that did not happen. It took further protracted litigation and the people had to struggle and voice their cause for restoring the criminal liability. Only the criminal liability was restored in 1991, leaving out the question of measly compensation, but again another two valuable years between 1989 and 1991 were lost and wrong impression had gone to the world at large that all this stood settled. On reopening the criminal liability, the plight of victims did not evoke that sympathy which was witnessed earlier. The case had gone under trial no doubt, but USA and the UCC clearly washed their hands off the catastrophe and they maintain that position till this day.

Still the judiciary took rather long time at every step instead of making good for the lost time to the extent it could. The Lower Court ultimately committed the case to Session's Court in 1992. Basically in commitment proceedings the Lower Court is not required to appreciate the evidence. It has only to see that the case is triable by the Session's Court and secondly it has to provide to the accused persons copies of all the documents deposited by the police on which the prosecution proposes to rely. After fulfilling the above two conditions the Lower Court has to transfer the case with entire record to the Session's Court that has jurisdiction for trial. All the requisite copies are furnished by the police along with the chargesheet and the court has only to deliver the same to the accused. This simple process should not have taken more than a week at the most, but still it took one full year. The delays occurred at every step even at the stages where there could be no reason or justification for the same.

At this stage in 1993, the CBI requested the MEA for extradition of Warren Anderson, but that was not agreed to by the ministry. When I came on the scene in 1994, the CBI had been insisting on the extradition and the correspondence was going on and the communication that I had mentioned was a link in that chain.

Coming back to the court trial, the Session's Court took one more year for framing the charges that was not a job of more than one or two weeks or a month at the most. The charges were framed in 1993, but the same were promptly challenged through a petition in the High Court. Basically the High Court should not have entertained any such request at that stage. In any case that was rejected in 1995, but again two more valuable years were lost. The accused then moved the Supreme Court in 1995 and filed an SLP for quashing the charge. Eminent advocates namely Ashok Desai represented Keshab Mahindra, Fali S Nariman represented Gokhale and Rajender Singh represented the other Indian accused persons. Warren Anderson and other accused from USA never bothered about investigation or trial proceedings. The pleas of the petitioners were partially but substantially accepted by the Apex Court on 13.09.1996 and the charge was diluted from Section 304 Part II to 304A IPC read with Section 35 of the same code. Now, the case was remanded to the Court of CJM who had authority to try the reduced offence of rash and negligence act u/s 304A IPC as it is triable by the Lower Court only. Full nine years were lost as the case returned to its position of 1.12.1987 to the CJM Court in 1996.

That made a fundamental difference to the case as it stood converted from a very serious to the most ordinary an offence. The CBI/Government should have taken it up for review, as scrutiny of the Supreme Court judgment offers enough scope for filing a Review Petition. As it is, apart from the issues of appreciation and non-appreciation of evidence on record, the judgment contradicts itself while discussing the crucial issue of the validity of Section 304 Part II and subsequently of Section 304A read with Section 35 IPC. I do not propose to go into the merits of the evidence but concentrate only on the internal contradiction in the Apex Court judgment that by itself is more than enough to compel any court to review this decision. Relevant excerpts from two parts of the same 1996 judgment of the Supreme Court are reproduced below that will bring home the contradiction beyond any doubt:

While dealing with applicability of Section 304 Part II IPC the court observed "... the material relied upon by the prosecution for framing a charge under Section 304 Part II must at least prima facie indicates that the accused had done an act which had caused death with at least such a knowledge that he was by such act likely to cause death. The entire material which the prosecution relied upon before the Trial Court for framing the charge cannot support such a charge unless it indicates prima facie that on that fateful night the plant was run by the concerned accused with the knowledge that such running of the plant was likely to cause death of human beings.

"Even assuming that it was a defective plant and was dealing with a very toxic and hazardous substance like MIC the mere act of storing such a material by the accused in tank could not even prima facie suggest that the concerned accused thereby had knowledge that they were likely to cause death to human beings. In our view the prosecution on the material as aforesaid had made out a prima facie case under Section 304A IPC ... consequently prima facie is made out for framing charges under Section 304A IPC." The judgment is clearly based on one single issue that there was lack of such knowledge on the part of workers/supervisors/management and such knowledge according to them was the crucial ingredient and this very crucial ingredient was missing, which was enough to throw out the case under Section 304 Part II.

They further made the following observations in examining if the same facts could constitute an offence under Section 304A read with 35 IPC for rash and negligent act in respect of the accused persons at S.No. 2, 3, 4 Keshab Mahindra, Chairman, Vijay Gokhale, MD and Kishore Kumar, VP UCIL who were at controlling level and also UCIL as a corporate body.

"So far as the accused Nos. 2, 3, 4 and 12 are concerned, the material produced on record clearly indicates at least prima facie that they being at the helm of affairs have to face this charge for the alleged negligence and rashness of their subordinates who actually operated the plant on that fateful night and for that purpose Section 35 of the IPC would also prima facie get attracted against them. A mere look at the Section shows that if the alleged act against the accused becomes criminal by the remaining accused who represented them on spot and who had to carry out their directions from them and who were otherwise required to supervise their activity. Section 35 of IPC could at least prima facie be invoked against accused 2, 3, 4 and 12 to be read with Section 304A IPC. Consequently on the material led by the prosecution against the accused at this stage prima facie case was made out by the prosecution for framing charges against 2, 3, 4 and 12 under Section 35 IPC."

The Supreme Court held that against the persons at controlling level charge stood under Section 304A read with Section 35 IPC "on account of their sharing common knowledge about the defective running of plant". It is obvious that the court itself has imputed knowledge to these officers as also the subordinates. The court, as is apparent from the above scrutiny, was asking for the same to hold them guilty under Section 304 Part II IPC but that however they could not see in that context but they themselves imputed the same in the other lesser context. Knowledge about a fact is something absolute. Either it is there or it is not. Context or the gravity of the offence makes no difference to that. But the moment the knowledge is imputed, the offence under Section 304 Part II IPC becomes complete. It was a patent error of appreciation on the part of the court. Even otherwise since in this case they have upheld Section 35 IPC which by itself presupposes knowledge or intention, there appears to be no reason to have discarded the same logic or the line of reasoning while dealing with Section 304 Part II. Section 35 IPC is reproduced below for ready appreciation of the reader.

> "Whenever an act, which is criminal only by reason of its being done with a criminal knowledge or intention, is done by several persons, each of such persons who joins in the act with such knowledge or intention is liable for the act in the same manner as if the act were done by him alone with that knowledge or intention."

Intention or knowledge is an essential ingredient of Section 35 IPC. If Supreme Court held accused 2, 3, 4 and 12 liable under Section 35 IPC, there is presumption or acknowledgement on the part of Supreme Court that these persons had knowledge that the plant was likely to be fatal under the conditions and circumstances it was designed and operating. It is clear that the Supreme Court itself has attributed existence of knowledge of likely fatality on the part of all those whom it has held liable for prosecution under Section 304A read with Section 35. But, the moment this knowledge is imputed, the same constitutes offence against them all under Section 304 Part II IPC as well. The Supreme Court while discussing the charge under Section 304 Part II precluded such or any knowledge on part of all the accused, but could not wish it out for Section 35 read with 304A IPC, thereby making all the qualitative difference and exposing them all to the offence under culpable homicide not amounting to murder, thereby exposing itself to taking contradictory line in the same case.

It is strange that since 1996 till 2010 when the Lower Court announced its judgment, no cognizance was ever taken of this fact and neither the Government, nor the CBI moved forward a review petition in this case. Actually CBI should have taken up the matter for filing review petition in the Supreme Court in 1996 itself. It was a fatal lapse, unlikely to happen in the CBI, as there is a very good and foolproof set procedure in CBI that every court judgment or direction in any case, irrespective of its seriousness or contents, is examined on the file from the legal angle as also from the angle of investigation with special reference to the former. Such an examination in this case also, would not have been missed by the CBI. But, as it is, the CBI cannot file any review petition or SLP on its own. Under the rules of business, it has to seek the approval of the Law Ministry through the Ministry of Personnel. All this is never missed in the CBI unless there is some prior indication from above. As such it can be safely presumed that the CBI must have moved the case after examination and proposed for filing of a review petition. But the fact is that such a petition was actually not filed. The issue requires to be looked into deeper. Justice

Ahmadi has also said now that if the judgment was not acceptable, why the Government/CBI did not move a review petition. He cannot justify his action by saying so, but the fact is that the petition was not filed which, in all fairness and as per the prevalent routine, should have been done. In CBI filing of or ignoring the filing of such a petition is a top level decision by the Director himself. Joginder Singh, who was the Director CBI in September 1996 can explain that as to whether it was his own decision or he was asked to do so or the Government had disagreed with his proposal if the same was referred to them. CBI records will also speak out whether CBI applied for or did not and if it did what was the response of the Ministry of Personnel and the Law Ministry. If the CBI did not approach the ministry, its files will surely speak out the reason for not doing so. Somebody has to be held accountable as it is fraught with risk in future also as it is a patent way to kill an important case like this one that as per media reports took a toll of no less than 5000 lives, besides rendering lacs of people perpetually sick.

There was another aspect, that Anderson never participated in any processes. The CBI had declared him an absconder and took up his extradition case with Ministry of External Affairs (MEA) as extradition under the treaty is their function. Correspondence had been going on between the MEA and the CBI for years, but the CBI did not leave it and kept pursuing for his extradition with the ministry.

The case was finally heard and formally decided by the CJM Court on 7th June 2010. The court awarded the maximum permissible punishment under the section of law for which the case was tried. The Trial Court could do no better as it was only *de jure* recognition of the *de facto* decision that had been virtually forced down by the Supreme Court in toning down the section of law. Even if the CJM found evidence enough for conviction for culpable homicide, not amounting to murder, he could neither enforce that punishment himself, nor could he send the case to a higher court as hands of all judiciary were tied by the Supreme Court judgment. However that raised the public outcry now in 2010 only as the punishment, by itself, was too little in the face of thousands of deaths, besides the life had become a living hell for another few lacs. Apart from the quantum of punishment, the people had not been looked after and the compensation had fallen much short of the requirements for survival and for getting treatment of the victims. There were countrywide protests.

It is strange that the Supreme Court judgment did not evoke any protests in 1996, though the case was practically decided then. Media also did not make any noise during these 14 long years. While Law Minister Veerappa Moily now said that the verdict was a "burial of justice" and Environment Minister Jairam Ramesh called it "unsatisfactory", and the opposition also cried foul, but why they chose to remain silent at the proper time in 1996 when the case was really scuttled by the Supreme Court judgment. If the CBI says it is satisfied with the court judgment "announcing maximum punishment for the accused under Section 304A IPC for which they were tried", it is right as it secured maximum punishment prescribed in Section 304A under which the trial was conducted as per the orders of the Apex Court.

Besides, the political parties which are fighting now, remained quiet for such a long period. All of them are guilty of neglecting the people, particularly when all the possible combinations of political parties were in power at the Centre, from time to time, but nobody raised voice at all. It is intriguing indeed. Now, when the milk is spilt, they are crying and the blame game goes on and on and the real issues will be lost and die down in the political controversies as this author observed in his book titled *Financial Terrorism: Black Money and the Indian Elite:* "Any issue that is desired to be killed, draw that into the quagmire of political polemics and be sure that it would be dumped as the nation would get tired of the spate of political wrangling and the people would regret why at all they raised it, even if the same may concern the most urgent matters of vital importance in everyday life or of lasting value."

Chapter - II

THE EXTRADITION DEBATE

The judgment shocked the nation as the punishment of two years in jail appeared to be too little for the offence of that immensity involving at least 5000 deaths and rendering lacs of others incapacitated, infirm, sick and helpless. Further the realisation that Anderson and all other foreigners and the corporate entities in India as well had gone scot-free, compounded the outrage. All these accompanied with the revelation that the MEA did not intend to put in serious efforts at his extradition brought nationwide protests to the fore and an endless debate ensued.

I had joined the CBI in April 1994 and handled this case from April 1994 to July 1995. At that time it was a dormant case as the chargesheet had already been filed long back in 1987 and only various fringe issues were coming up before the court at Bhopal and these were being dealt with in the CBI as well. A chargesheeted case normally goes dormant as there is nothing to be done in it on day to day basis and this case was at that stage. It came up either on the date of trial or on the question of pursuing matters related to extradition of Warren Anderson or such like other matters. The only incident worth mentioning in this case that I can recall after 16 years, occurred during my tenure of 15 months when I handled this case, pertained to a communication that was received from the MEA asking the CBI not to pursue the extradition case of Anderson. The same was dealt with on the file in routine; the CBI did not agree with the suggestion and replied back accordingly that we could not drop the same as Anderson was the prime accused. However correspondence on this issue had been going on for quite some time, ever since the request for his extradition was filed with MEA in 1993, and also it continued later after my departure from the scene of this case.

After pronouncement of the judgment by the CJM Court on 7th June 2010, the media started approaching me because one journalist Tim Edward, as mentioned earlier, had put my conversation about the case with him on the Internet. When various channels/press people approached me, I confirmed the receipt of such a communication asking us not to pursue the extradition case of Anderson.

My statement came on air on 8th morning and by noon the two Union Ministers Moily and Salman Khurshid were vociferously denying the existence of any such communication or existence of any pressure on CBI. The fact is that they did not have any time in which they could have checked the old record of 15-16 years in MEA or in the CBI in a matter of just an hour or two, whereas I had made a specific reference that the communication was received and was dealt with on the CBI files. It was just a blind denial being forced down the throat by both of them as neither was holding the relevant portfolio now and Moily was never concerned either with the MEA or with the CBI. He had neither the knowledge nor the rationale to have reacted. However the situation changed the next day when evidence started tumbling out. The first to come out was Moti Singh, the then DM of Bhopal in 1984. He joined the fray and stated that they were asked by the Chief Secretary to bail out Anderson immediately and escort him honourably to the airport. Further, the then head of civil aviation department of MP Government joined the issue stating clearly that he was asked by the CM Secretariat to make the personal plane of the CM available and ready to fly to Delhi immediately. According to him, the identity of the prospective flyer was not disclosed to him. He came to know about the foreign dignitary as the VIP, only after Anderson appeared on the scene at the airport duly escorted by the two top officials of the district. That brought the line to the then Chief Minister Arjun Singh, taking it away from the civil servants. Arjun Singh was contacted by the media as he had been maintaining absolute silence so far, but now he had to break it and stated that the law and order situation of Bhopal at that time was deteriorating fast and violence against Anderson was expected to erupt. As a preventive measure he had no option but to release Anderson and to evacuate him. He also reiterated that he had made similar statement in 1984 also that Anderson was bailed and escorted out to save the city of Bhopal from violence.

It is prima facie absolutely a wrong and an erroneous view as at no stage was there any evidence on the ground that people were turning violent till 7th of December or the people of Bhopal had any clue about the visit of Anderson or they were bothered about him. The people of Bhopal were under heavy shock and high anxiety. In such a devastating disaster or personal crisis, the psychologists say that one does not turn violent initially. The human mind proceeds from one to the other stage step by step. Psychologically shock and high anxiety constitute the first phase followed by the denial phase that nothing has happened. The realisation about the circumstances and the surroundings dawns upon them when they cannot wish it out and realize that the tragedy had really hit them and denial is of no consequence. It is at this stage that the violent phase takes over but all this would have taken a week or more. People of Bhopal on 7th morning were still passing through the first phase. There were no signs of violence at that time and also no such reference to violence has appeared in any of the accounts other than that of Arjun Singh. People were still taking stock and were busy with the dead, arranging for the disposal of their bodies and fending for treatment of the surviving victims as also of their own.

There is still another angle that if there were any violence or any was expected, it should have flared up immediately with the release of Anderson and rather subsided with the arrest. So long as he was under arrest, people were assured that action was being taken and arrest was the first serious step. It is the release that should have infuriated the people to violence and not the arrest. But the fact is that being under strong shock they were not able even to protest and much less prepared to cause any violence even on release of Anderson.

It is absolutely wrong and has also been proved so by the later events that Anderson was not released on account of deteriorating law and order situation, whatever be the other reasons. There is another aspect that if violence was expected in Bhopal, Anderson could have been advised not to visit Bhopal or after arrest he could have been shifted to any other part of the country. Under the law, various options were available and bailing out an accused of the crime within a few hours was not the appropriate alternative.

Further, are our governments so week that they cannot handle the after-effects of arrest of a person accused of a criminal offence? If so everyone of substance will create a situation and get relief. It is a most illogical excuse taken by the then CM, which is not at all tenable.

After the head of the civil aviation department of Madhya Pradesh Government, Digvijay Singh was the next to jump into the fray, defending the State Government of which he was also the CM for a full decade. He was abroad at that time and his statement came from there only. He threw the ball back into the court of the Centre from where the Union Ministers had been trying to push it hard into the court of the State. However, like Arjun Singh withdrawing the order of arrest in 2-3 hours, Digvijay Singh also turned wiser immediately and had to withdraw his statement indicting the Centre, before long. But he had already given out his version. Every political leader looked at and reacted to the events first from the angle of his own survival and political prospects and secondly that of his party. It was absolutely clear that they did not have any concern or regard for the facts of the case, the law of the land or the suffering of the people. Had Digvijay Singh not remained the CM of the State, without batting an eyelid, he would also have joined the chorus with others throwing the entire blame solely on the State?

Arun Nehru, a Union Minister in 1984 and a close confidant of Rajiv Gandhi, the then Prime Minister, tried to make some clarifications. Following the general pattern, he agreed with the Central leaders that it was the prerogative of the State to have bailed Anderson out, but at the same time he also contended that Anderson after flying from Bhopal on 7th evening had met the President and the Home Minister in Delhi. Does that not make it clear that the trip of Anderson was a sponsored and pre-arranged one and that he was guest of the Central Government. Otherwise, an impromptu meeting with the President is not easy or possible for a businessman whatever be his standing as lots of formalities have to be gone into before any appointment with the President can be fixed, unless Anderson was so important that all programmes, protocol and procedures had to be relaxed to accommodate him. If centre attached so much importance, it is quite natural that it would restrain the State from the audacity of arresting him. A further question arises that since he was accused of causing such a massive destruction of human life, should he be allowed to meet the President at all. Why he met the President and the Home Minister and what did he discuss needs to be made public. People are certainly entitled to know. He was accorded a bigger than life size honour by the Centre. The State Chief Minister who had unwittingly arrested such an honourable VVIP, would have looked stupid to himself. It appears the State arrested him in utter ignorance or as it appeared in some sections of the media, may be Arjun Singh arrested him to mop up the political gains at the forthcoming elections and to show how benevolent and sympathetic the Government of Madhya Pradesh under him was to the sufferings of the people. It is a different matter that the CM had to go back on his decision.

The stream of people proving the truth that fortunately got initiated with me on 8th morning was growing rather fast. Gordan Streeb who was charge de affairs of the American Embassy in December 1984 was the next to jump into the fray. He spoke from USA from the university in which he is teaching now. In the telephonic interview that was widely aired by various TV channels, he stated that Anderson was promised safe passage through India in advance before he embarked on his journey to this country in the aftermath of Bhopal tragedy. According to him they were surprised that despite assurances to the contrary by the Government of India, he was arrested on landing at Bhopal. Streeb goes on stating that after getting information about the arrest of Anderson on 7th December from Bhopal from the Americans accompanying him from embassy, he (Streeb) took up the issue with the MEA at Delhi and arranged the release of Anderson. Quickly Rasgotra, the then Foreign Secretary by and large confirmed what had been disclosed by Streeb. By now it was established well that it was all under the orders of Centre and the Centre was in the loop for every step that was taken by the State for his release. That incidentally had determined the mindset of the bureaucracy as happens day in and day out that bureaucrats work, shape their views and take action according to their mindset which, as stated earlier, is determined by the line the bosses in the Government have indicated or taken.

Whatever Streeb said prima facie appeared to be fresh revelation, but all this affair of assurances was known in Delhi to scribes and GK Reddy of *The Hindu* had filed a report about central assurances as early as 7th December 1984 itself that appeared as front page story in *The Hindu* on 8th December 1984. He wrote "...Mr Gordan Streeb called on the Foreign Secretary Mr MK Rasgotra to voice the US Government's concern over Mr Anderson's arrest despite the assurances of safe passage given by the Indian Government when he offered to fly to Bhopal". How can Reddy file story about assurances on 7th December, if there were none. That utterly falsifies the claims made by Arjun Singh, the then CM, that he released Anderson in the interest of maintenance of peace in Bhopal.

It is clear that Anderson left USA on 6th in order to reach India on 7th. Assurances were arranged in advance that might have taken another day or more. It is obvious that the assurances might have been negotiated on 5th or earlier. The Central Government would have extended these assurances after due consideration. Who confirmed these assurances to the Americans and Anderson, is of no consequence, but were obviously well considered by the Government in the MEA. It is at this stage that his Delhi programme for 7th would also have been fixed in advance. There can be no proof but these are the natural deductions and logical conclusions that automatically follow from the attendant circumstances.

Though the decision to arrest Anderson was that of the State Chief Minister, but to release him appears to be that of the Central Government. Streeb spoke to the Foreign Secretary who in turn would take orders from the Foreign Minister who could only have taken the decision, but since arrest in a case of crime was the subject matter of the Home Ministry, PV Narsimha Rao as Home Minister might have been entrusted the job to convey the Government decision to the Chief Minister. There is otherwise no way how could Home Minister have intruded into the territory of another ministry on his own. Such interference is highly resented by the other ministries and in any case is not a done thing.

Now my disclosure made at the outset about the communication from MEA fits very well and falls firmly in place in the scheme of things set by the Centre at the highest level. Since that was the decision taken at the highest level, how could the officials in the ministry take up the extradition case later on in 1994-95, the period to which my statement pertained? In view of our repeated insistence in writing, the advice to us in the communication was naturally in that light, though we were not aware of this development as the communication did not explain the same in details. All that we knew from the correspondence was that it was all a part of the bilateral relations.

The media in its enquiry also approached the then CBI Director K Vijay Rama Rao on 8th June 2010 to confirm about the communication I had referred to. Rama Rao, as per media reports, initially denied any knowledge about it, but the next day when he appeared on the channel with me, he stated that if "Lall had put up some such papers as he says, I would have approved", but he could not remember the same at this distance of time. He also made a reference to the long and protracted correspondence on the question of extradition but denied specific knowledge about such communication. If not about this issue, what correspondence had CBI to undertake with the MEA on Bhopal Gas case? The CBI applied for extradition in 1993, if ministry had supported us and taken up our request with the US Government, there was no reason for the CBI to have entered into the protracted correspondence. The occasion arose only when the MEA raised queries in place of agreeing to and pursuing our request. The MEA was perhaps being pulled by the CBI and the US authorities on the opposite sides and the diplomatic/political decisions of the Government were impinging on it from above, that made matters difficult for it. Such differences and official disagreements as existed between the MEA and the CBI, on the question of pursuing the extradition of Anderson or going slow on it or dropping it altogether, happen now and then and are not treated as big issues. Somehow a great fuss was raised on this little fact coming out and that focussed the limelight, so much so that the Union Ministers had to rush in and try to bulldoze the issue by blanket denials, that too without any verification or knowledge.

Incidentally some press reports mentioned about Joginder Singh, the Director CBI from August 1996 onwards, mentioning that in a high level meeting of Secretaries presided over by the then Cabinet Secretary and attended by him as Director CBI, it was stated that the extradition matter of Anderson may not be pressed. It must have happened after the Supreme Court decision in 1996. It is appreciable that the ministry continuously maintained its stand. If that could be deliberated in the meeting, what is the big deal about sending a communication conveying the same two years earlier?

Now, when everything has fallen into place, the public may see how pressures and even intimidation are let loose if anyone speaks out the truth that is not palatable or acceptable to the powers that be. The moment my statement became public, without verification or going into the records, the strong reactions started flowing from no less than two serving Union Ministers namely Salman Khurshid and Veerappa Moily and another former minister RK Dhawan. The attitudes of the latter two in particular were even threatening and abusive. Some of their statements are listed below:

The Law Minister said "the former CBI officer should have taken a stand and insisted on Anderson's extradition."

The then Minister of State for External Affairs Salman Khurshid remarked: "How can the Ministry of External Affairs give any advice to the CBI. The ministry does not do so."

Moily, the Law Minister thundered: "After retirement, many people can give many statements. I don't have any comments on that. And any responsible officer taking an excuse that he has been interfered with is absolutely an irresponsible statement and it is not done at all. And you know not at this point of time and at this distance of time he has to realise this kind of big enlightenment taking place with an investigative officer. I think we need to do something to deal with such people who will not discharge their duties, failed to discharge their duty and after retirement try to become heroes or martyrs of the situation."

S Rajarathinam commented on web: "The statement of Mr Lall after his retirement from service is highly deplorable. Why he did not open this matter while he was in service? Perhaps he also wanted to curry favour from his higher-ups! Had he resigned from service, declaring that his hands are tied up in arresting Anderson—perhaps there would have been a revolt and agitation by people of Bhopal creating law & order problem for MP Government? I feel Mr Lall is also a party to the delayed verdict and he can be charged under the case of "Suppressio veri" while in service and "suggestio falsi" after retirement. I do not know why these retired IPS officers come out with Dutch courage statement after retirement. Anyway this clearly confirm the statement of Thedore Roosevelt that in India "Man is born free but he is always in chains."

The first statement of the Law Minister that I should have taken a stand meaning thereby that I did not take a stand, is absolutely devoid of facts. CBI files even now would be witness to the stand that I took in this case. Has the Law Minister cared to check the files or he presumed that he knew everything under the sun. Whosoever heard me over the TV channels knows that I clearly stated that I did not agree with the command of the Government, opposed it tooth and nail on file and it was primarily due to my initiative that the CBI took the stand and opposed the missive in question as an organisation and replied back to the Government accordingly. So the CBI and myself took a strong stand consistently and whatever he says I should have done, was actually done without leaving out anything. Further action lay in the MEA and nobody else could do anything more. Problem is that reaction of Veerappa Moily was impromptu without knowing or ascertaining the facts giving an impression as if he was duty bound to say irrespective of the facts of the matter. The fact is that as Law Minister now, he cannot be privy to any knowledge nor he has any locus standi to comment. I may introduce him to the routine in the Government or for that matter in any organisation. The correspondence goes on; one may agree or may not agree, the differences keep on arising and these are thrashed out or the junior organisations keep on telling the seniors who make their own choice on what line be pursued. Pursuing extradition of Anderson or not doing so in national interest is the prerogative of the sovereign power, but then the reasons have to be recorded and explained to the people and all this has to be in the public domain at least after lapse of some time. All such limits of time have been crossed. It all became relevant only after the judgment and people have a right to know everything now. Mistakes committed at the Government level need to be exposed and acknowledged gracefully, every human being can commit bona fide mistakes. A civil servant does not go to public or take to streets after writing every note or communication where there are differences, but when the consequences lead to some catastrophe, that too at the national level, these differences become relevant and then the healthy nation analyses them to find where the things had gone wrong. That is the proper time to come out publicly for all concerned. At the same time it is an exercise to hold the people accountable and lay down the rules of the game for future. There was no occasion for me to have gone public for receiving such a communication, or for having taken a stand against and for sending a reply to that effect from the CBI at that stage.

Second statement from Salman Khurshid raises the question of jurisdiction that the MEA cannot give any direction to CBI. Salman Khurshid who had been minister in the MEA knows very well that extradition is a subject of the MEA and it is their function to deal with other Governments and CBI could only request the MEA. It is up to the MEA to take whatever action they may like. The CBI could only request and oppose the actions proposed by the MEA and all that was done.

The third is a long statement by Moily, but basically the minister has charged me with coming out after retirement and has accused me of not discharging my duties while in service. Unfortunately, the case has been decided after my retirement. I can assure Moily that if I were in service, then also I would have spoken the same language and the same sentiment as I have done all through my service. I have retired, should I subvert national interest by keeping quiet. No, Mr Moily, NOT at ALL. If he cares for facts and truth, he can verify my stand from records in CBI that are replete with similar notings from me. For his information, in the Jain Hawala case, I had demanded to carry out complete investigations, including searches of the premises of the then PM and of the former PM at which I was removed from the zone dealing with the case. I did not suffer it silently, as Moily now suggests, I then protested in very clear terms, through my DO letter dated 1.8.95 (Appendix - II), to the Director mentioning clearly that the CBI was not allowed to investigate cases against the high and mighty in general and I was not being allowed to investigate the then PM and other bigwigs. For the information of Moily and Rajarathinam, I was very much in service at that time. He does not know or realise or try to ascertain about what sort of a person he is commenting upon and accusing. Instead of omnibus comments in the vacuum, will he dare to check facts and after that can Mr Moily discuss the issue with me threadbare on any TV channel that he may choose. I would welcome if he could be able to suggest what else could I or the CBI do beyond what was done. However all the observations or remarks that he or I make should be fortified with facts. Incidentally, I may add that the CBI files that I dealt with are full of my notes of dissent. There would be no week when on matter of principle, I would not have recorded dissent at least once. I stayed in CBI for 140 weeks, so Mr Moily can search the files and see for himself that I took stand for at least 100 times. He is in authority and files may not be beyond him or he can make the files available to me and I will sort out and show to him.

A vast number of reactions have appeared on the web of which very very few have criticised me whereas most of them have appreciated my stand and taken Mr Moily to task. The most severe criticism is from one S Rajarathinam who goes on making accusations and thereby betraying his lack of knowledge and understanding about the facts in issue. His first accusation is why I did not open up while in service. It has been amply demonstrated that all possible actions were taken and the stand of the Government was opposed wherever required. He asks for my resignation. Let me make him wiser that I have been fighting such battles since my probation days till the close of my service and saw 31 transfers during my service. Does he want only yes men to remain in service and voice of sanity, the truth and the law to disappear from the scene altogether? I am a fighter and not an escapist. Resigning, in my view, is running away like a coward. I fought pitched battles which is beyond the imagination or comprehension of the people of the calibre of Rajarathinam as it appears from his observations. Actually internal cleansing and internal fight is more difficult but that is essential and indispensable and I waged that all through, of which he is completely ignorant or too committed to appreciate or understand some other view than his own. Besides, if after my retirement I were to say that during service I had compulsion to commit wrong, then only I will lay open to what Moily says. But I always opposed all wrong commands and now I am only placing it before the people that how pressures are exercised and how I opposed the same successfully and did not give in. Why he wants to silence the people like me who want to expose their wrong, illegal and immoral ways. His strain again was the same in the case of Pratyush Sinha, the CVC, who recounted his experience at the time of his retirement in September. He can recount them on his retirement only. Why Moily is out to gag every inconvenient view not palatable to him. As the

Union Law Minister he should rather think of reforming the system, the procedures, the routine and the personnel rather than taking upon himself of killing every voice of sanity. I have explained in details how I performed my job more than expected, but is he (Moily) doing his duty? Has he amended the anti-corruption laws, has he found some ways and means to expedite judicial trials. He better concentrate on his own job rather than throwing irrelevant comments left and right.

Further, it appears that before commenting on me, he did not watch the TV or read press reports and took to blind bullying. He (as also Rajarathinam) accuses me of letting Anderson go. He is terribly ignorant of the fact that I joined CBI 10 years after release of Anderson on bail. I was not on the scene when Anderson was arrested and bailed out. That happened in 1984 and I came to CBI in 1994. My only concern in this case was the extradition of Anderson. This has been repeated again and again. Use of hyperboles by him as reproduced on the earlier pages is no argument. I draw his attention to my article on CBI that appears as Appendix - I to the first chapter stating clearly that we were not allowed to investigate the big people. I was very much in the CBI at that time, but had courage to write. What else? If Rajarathinam is sincere to the nation he needs to tender public apology for his remarks. The same is true for Moily as well, as he accuses me of letting Anderson go. He is taking blind shots without regard to the fact as stated above, that the arrest of Anderson is an issue of 1984 whereas I entered CBI full ten years later in 1994. Where is the relevance of all that he spoke.

Moily kept on accusing people blindly left and right whosoever spoke a word that was different from his line of thinking or say contrary to his views. As per press reports PC Alexander, who was a close confidant of Indira Gandhi and also Rajiv Gandhi and had also served as Principal Secretary with the latter, spoke on the subject suggesting that the then Prime Minister may have had a role in the release of former Union Carbide chief Warren Anderson, accused in Bhopal Gas case. Law Minister Veerappa Moily mounted an attack on him. If Alexander or anyone else speaks out a word not to the liking of Moily, that person immediately becomes culpable. What a law (principle) propounded by the Hon'ble Law Minister.

Law Minister, it appears, has that habit. As touched upon a little earlier, his recent severe outburst has been against Pratyush Sinha, the outgoing CVC. As per media reports, Pratyush at his retirement while interacting with the media, gave out his assessment that only thirty per cent of the Government servants are honest. Moily let loose the same tirade that why is he stating so after his retirement? When else should he give his overall impression if not at the time of his retirement? There could not have been more appropriate an occasion and the Law Minister should have drawn lesson from vast experience in the field of the outgoing CVC and implemented his suggestions. Moreover, in my view, Pratyush has been too liberal. If only we had thirty per cent honest public servants, corruption would not have been that rife and conditions around the country would not have been so chaotic. What message the minister wants to send? Unless officers who dealt with such matters choose to speak out, there would be no progress. Does the Law Minister want this mess to continue? Why as Law Minister he has not created an infrastructure and legal framework for fighting corruption? Our agencies may be treated and equipped legally as per the norms of the civilised world. CBI and other investigating agencies need be freed from the yoke of the executive, both the political and the bureaucratic. Laws of corruption need be updated and freed from the colonial hang up of protecting the loyalist, howsoever corrupt he may be. There can be no place for the provisions for permission to investigate under Section 26 CVC Act and for prosecution sanction under Section 19 of the PC Act. Besides, he should ensure the organisation and functioning of the courts in such a way that the time under trial is cut down. Mr Moily should better concentrate on his job, where there are innumerable holes, rather than pouncing upon and intimidating everyone who utters even a word that may not be to his liking.

Moily was unstoppable and made the following statement that it was a culpable act on my part to have allowed Anderson to go. He went on further to challenge my integrity and heap adverse comments left and right. He appeared more like a mafia goon punishing one who said something against him or which he thought was against his master or the gang. For sometime it appeared that rule of law did not exist in the land and the freedom of speech had been given a go-by despite its continuance on the holy book, the Constitution of India. Now, what I had said initially has been corroborated from all sides and the latest development has finally brought forth the truth authentically from the horse's mouth itself. Some activists had filed applications under RTI with the CBI as also with the MEA for providing copy of the communication from MEA to CBI that I (BR Lall) had referred to. One such applicant Ajay K Agarwal has received the reply from DIG Rakesh Tyagi of CBI. Agarwal on my request has forwarded a copy of the same to me. The operative part of which reads "...it is intimated that the information sought by you is related to case no. RC 3/84(S)-CU-I. This case is still pending prosecution vis-a-vis Mr Warren Anderson, who is an absconder in the case. I am convinced the disclosure of information as asked by you would impede the process of pending extradition and prosecution. Therefore the information sought by you is denied...." A copy of this communication appears on the next page:

No. 288/5/DIG/AC-I/RTI/10/51.
O/o the Dy. Inspr. Genl. of Police,
CBI, AC-I, 7th floor,
Block No. 3, CGO Complex,
Lodhi Road, New Delhi- 03
Dated: 05/07/2010

To

Shri Ajay K Agrawal,
r/o F-1, Jangpura Extension,
New Delhi - 110014.

Sub: Request dt. 08.05.2008 for information under RTI Act, 2005 - reg.

Sir,

May please refer to your letter dt. 09.06.2008 addressed to the Director, CBI, New Delhi.

2. In this regard it is intimated that the information sought by you is related to case no. RC3/84 (S) - ACU - I. This case is still pending prosecution vis-a-vis Mr. Warren Anderson, who is an absconder in the case. I am convinced the disclosure of information as asked by you would impede the process of his pending extradition and prosecution. Therefore, the information sought by you is denied under section 8 (1) (h) of RTI Act, 2005.

4. In case you want to make an appeal against this decision of the undersigned. You can prefer an appeal u/s 19 of the RTI Act, 2005 within 30 days. The name and address of the Appellate Authority is Shri H.C. Awasthy, IPS. Joint Director, CBI. Anti-Corruption (HQ), 3rd Floor, Block No. 4, CGO Complex, Lodhi Road, New Delhi – 110003 (Tel. No. 24363586, e-mail ID : jdac1del@cbi.gov.in.

Yours faithfully,

Sd/-

(RAKESH AGGARWAL)
HEAD OF BRANCH/CPIO

The points to be noted are that the existence of such communication from MEA is admitted, but only the copy cannot be given, for whatever reasons. Had there been no such communication as stated by the ministers, the CBI would have simply denied the very receipt or the existence of the document? The claim that I made, stands admitted by the CBI itself. Why did the ministers not care to check with the CBI? Had they done so, they would not have made the wild and false accusations and the irresponsible remarks. I shudder at the thought if these were deliberate with full knowledge of facts. What they have to say now? Their misplaced concept about bulldozing everything that is unpleasant to them, in utter disregard of facts, does not behove their exalted stature as the Hon'ble ministers of this biggest democracy of the world? These are some of the questions that come to the mind of an ordinary person who has witnessed the scenario with some interest.

Strangest and most reckless response was from the professional, Joginder Singh, who had been Director CBI at one stage. In an interview, published in a daily newspaper on 21st June 2010 Joginder Singh has tried to malign me with absolutely incorrect facts that will not even require any comments as the reader will see for himself. The interviewer put to him the following question: "BR Lall stated that a letter came to him from MEA not to press extradition case of Warren Anderson. Did it come to your notice." Joginder Singh is stated to have replied: "Lall was too junior a functionary and MEA would not have written to him but to the Director and that Lall may be saying so to steal publicity." Like politicians, his statement is equally in disregard to the facts as also to the timing. From day one, I have been saying that I handled this case from April 1994 to July 1995. This has not only been repeated in the TV channels time and again, but has also appeared in the print media. Joginder Singh should have read or at least heard it so many times that my statement pertains to 1994-95, whereas he came to CBI in August 1996 only. How could he have seen or received such a communication in 1994-95? Secondly I never said that the communication was directly addressed to me or delivered to me. Even this has been clarified over the TV and settled when Rama Rao, who was the Director CBI at the crucial juncture in 1994-95, and myself appeared together on one TV channel. Rama Rao stated that so many communications were exchanged between MEA and the CBI, that even if such a communication were received, he could not have remembered offhand. He clearly stated over the TV that if Lall says that he had "put up to me, I might have approved the reply in routine." I had stated over the TV that I had put up the file to him. Since it was an ordinary communication and not a DO letter, there is no question of Director necessarily receiving it. Normally as per routine, the receipt clerk of the CBI should have received it and put it up through the office assistant and so on. JD is too high a functionary to receive the ordinary Dak personally, what to speak of the Director. It was put up to me on file and I further put up the same to the Director with my observations. Statement of Joginder Singh is factually wrong, misleading and misplaced and besides he was not on the scene of CBI till one to two years after this event, but God knows or only he can explain why he must make false, motivated and unverified statements, though he is supposed to be a professional that too unconnected with the incident. Need I comment who is seeking publicity?

Very recently Sh SK Datta, former Director CBI (in 1992-93) has published his memoirs in his book titled "*CBI Top Cop Recalls*," dealing with the subject of virtual government veto against the proposal for extradition of Anderson in the Bhopal Gas case as early as 1993 an year earlier to my account. He states that the Principal Secretary to the then PM called him to his office and virtually took him (Datta) to task for pressing the issue regarding extradition of Anderson. Incidentally CBI had made the move in 1993 only, so it was desired at the highest level to avoid his extradition. An excerpt from his book is reproduced which makes things absolutely clear “The CBI used to resist any interference in the investigation or during the trial of cases. As Director I was called to meet the Principal Secretary to the Prime Minister. He was almost furious and wanted to know why the CBI was proceeding against Anderson, an accused of the Bhopal Gas Leak case. He said that by doing so we were preventing foreign investment.” There can be no doubt now that not only the MEA, but also the PMO was also against taking any step for extradition of Anderson. This also is a pointer that PMO was controlling the matters related to his extradition and that explains everything else. Incidentally the statement brings out clearly how pressures were exerted on the CBI and the process of investigation hindered in routine. There does not appear any sanctity or seriousness either towards the people of Bhopal, their suffering, national interest or any other consideration for Indians or their self respect, but only international relations. This attitude of the PMO explains completely why that sell out bargain had to be entered into ignoring all the national interests. Anderson was such a big man so the proverbial pressure on CBI would also be proportionately high. Now that it is well established and admitted that such a letter, as I had claimed, has been received, will the ministers have courage and decency to offer a public apology. They certainly will if what they said was under the bona fide, though mistaken belief. But they will not if it was a calculated move to deliberately and maliciously malign the truth.

So much about the ministers. What should I expect from Joginder Singh as apology is too little an expectation from the highest police professional, the chief investigator (i.e. the collector of facts) of the country at one time?

Appendix – II

Central Bureau of Investigation

D.O. No. 79/AJD(N)/CBI/95

GOVERNMENT OF INDIA

C.G.O. COMPLEX, BLOCK NO.3

LODHI ROAD

NEW DELHI-110003

Dated August 1, 1995

B. R. LALL

JOINT DIRECTOR (NORTH)

Dear Shri Rao,

I am grateful to you for sounding me in advance on 19th regarding my transfer. Nobody has a title to any post and one has to serve wherever posted. Some people get attached to certain posts but as I told you that day, I have never clung to any post, but only upheld the principles wherever I have served with the result that during the 24½ years, since I was promoted as SP, this is my 26th transfer, that too despite the fact that I spent 12 years in 3 so-called insignificant postings (where one's straightforwardness does not hurt others), i.e. 3 years in ITBP, 4 years as SP (Vigilance) and 5 years as director NEPA. If these 3 posts and 12 years are taken away, it is my 23rd posting in a total period of 12½ years. Every time, the transfer was on a principled stand, which I took without bending.

2. During last few days, I have been hearing that during the period of last one month, when you decided to disassociate me and the Special director from the Hawala case, you have been mentioning that nothing was done in the Hawala case till the last month when yourself directly took over the case which precisely is on 26.6.1995. This mention was made before the IOs even.

3. Fact remains that it is I who introduced PC Act angle in the Hawala case, I brought the concept of kickbacks in projects much before interrogation of Jains as I developed my information sources in various institutions dealing with power projects and got lots of information. My staff fully cooperated and worked day and night including all ranks from DIG down to constable or a clerk. I myself, examined Kawas project first of all, supervised the interrogation of Jains which yielded valuable information. I am referring in particular to the statement of SK Jain, which has been thoroughly corroborated to the extent we could look into for further verification. I am always very frank while discussing with my juniors as also the seniors, but at the same time, carried out all the orders and jobs assigned to me and my organisation by yourself. I was however, in favour of looking into the massive record first before we convert the PE into an RC so that we have the evidence of payments and receipts, which is something primary for making out a case. But somehow we could not wait because of the pressure of Supreme Court and had to convert it into an RC a little premature but that was beyond our control.

4. It is also correct that the Supreme Court every time came heavy on us but for that the responsibility squarely rests with S.G.I. who as our Counsel should

have had complete knowledge of Law and should have been a master of facts but he has neither the knowledge nor the understanding of criminal laws and nor the capability to project whatever is told to him. He would not marshal all the facts before the Hon'ble court. The other factor has been no investigation for a little over 2 years between 1991 to 1993, for which Supreme Court holds CBI responsible. Though CBI as an institution is indefensible for this delay, but actually none of us is individually responsible as none of us was there at the scene at that time in this case.

5. It is correct that scrutiny of records was rather slow and I was myself not satisfied, but it was because I had very limited staff and during last almost an year, despite my requests verbally and in writing, not even one person could be added to Anti-Corruption II though it is normal for investigation of such a scam. Now full one DIG with an SP and 6 IOs were added through ACB/Delhi. I could not supplement from ACI as they are also deep in investigation of Assam LOC scam which also has huge dimensions and for that also I got only one extra IO. All through this time, I worked with 50 to 60% vacancies of Inspectors in my charge. I could never spare more than 2 to 3 IOs, except when SK Jain, JK Jain etc. were being interrogated, when I put the entire AC II on this job. Chronologically earlier as directed by the Supreme Court from September to December, the staff was busy in interrogating the 115 persons whose names were found entered in diaries. From January, the exercise of collecting the documents of various projects in which Jains' had worked and subsequently, the verification into the PE started and after conversion of PE into RC, on 4.3.1995, the searches, arrest and interrogation

of Jains started which continued round the clock till 20.3.1995. After that, we prepared for the Supreme Court where matters relating to bails and arrests of Jains, came up and we started running into courts and arranging for arrest of NK Jain and BR Jain. There were Supreme Court hearings on 27.3.95, 2.4.95, 18.4.95, 2.5.95, however, we kept on working overtime collecting records, examining projects, verifying statements of Jains and also arrested NK Jain after getting him from UK. It was only after 2.5.95 that we could heave a sigh of relief, as ACII directly under Amod and closely supervised by me had been working for long hours into the night foregoing their leave and holidays. How can one say that no work was done? We carried out every aspect of investigation as desired by yourself and also whatever occurred to us. Your further directions by that time were also received regarding conduct of investigations which was impossible if my team was not strengthened by diverting entire staff of ACII to this case. As such, on 4.5.95, leaving only 4/5 IOs in the other 3 branches, I diverted entire strength of ACII to Hawala case and divided them into 3 teams each under an SP, Shri MP Singh and Shri Mukesh Sahay were to examine the projects and team under Shri HS Sandhu, SP was to collect field information and conduct field enquiries into various persons mentioned in diaries in order to fix their identity and to collect the evidence of payment/ receipt by them, including the evidence regarding their assets, their families, etc. Work picked up very fast and we located evidence in Kawas, questionable nexus in Uri and Dulhasti projects but which still required deeper probe. Slowly, we were progressing to close on some of the big guns in particular as statements of SK Jain and JK Jain were getting verified. In May when Amod was suddenly repatriated from the scene it did slow down the work as the feeling went round that he has been removed. I talked to the IOs and SPs and brought them out of their frustration, but about a week was lost. Amod K Kanth was perceived by the staff as an honest and straightforward officer, but by sudden repatriation, whereas earlier his willingness and my recommendations had been sought by Administration Division of CBI, the message went home that straightforwardness is at a discount even in CBI.

6. Yourself held detailed discussion, during the week with various SPs and discussions with Shri HS Sandhu were awaited when in last week of June, I was removed from the scene and yourself took over the work of supervising the IOs directly and started discussing about chargesheeting some public servants. Even the SDCBI was by and large ignored in subsequent discussions. The question of chargesheet had come up with me also but I brought it to the notice of DCBI that :

    a. There was as yet no evidence regarding receipt of payments made to the persons named in Diary.

    b. Evidence of motive was yet to come.

    c. Evidence of favours shown and irregularities committed was coming in, which had to be developed and put in right perspective.

    d. For unearthing further evidence and the assets searches were also required in particular of the big fish as they were emerging the main culprits.

7. All through, I have been of the opinion and still hold that if it was not possible to chargesheet the big fish, as different standards are supposed to be adopted

in their cases, then we should forget about the small ones also. For, this scandal originated from kickbacks, which were created forced on this country and were perpetuated by the big ones including the Ministers and Prime Minister. Chargesheeting minor functionaries only, for receiving fringe benefits of the scam would amount to a cover up of the scam itself. I will come to this question again in detail a little later.

8. The DCBI started avoiding me and broke the hierarchical chain and I became a subject of denigration before my own subordinates. I may not bother for my own sake but, the chain of command was breaking, and the wrong signals were being transmitted. Incidentally, during 3 weeks since then till 18th, only the existing information has been compiled. It was something known, and established only the identity. The further scrutiny stopped, the experts who had been called, had to be dropped for the time being. I was planning this work some 10 days later, as sitting day and night where I would also have participated with the staff, this compilation would take 3-4 days only and in the meantime, I was searching for further evidence as early as possible to find some evidence regarding payments/receipt/motives/ favours. The contents of all the diaries and documents brought in the searches of March '95 were personally known to me as I had glanced through most of them when these were initially brought. These contained only the routine information of telephone numbers. One diary had repeated mention to MPN and flat for MPN. It is from this diary that Jain in interrogation identified him as MP Narayan and we reached the Neyaveli Lignite and the Coal sector. These only helped in establishing identity. It was a minor matter as compared to evidence of motive, favours, payments etc. and moreover it

required very little time. However, we work as a team according to the directions of the director. Had director told me about his priority, I would have got the compilation work done. There would be no need to ignore me or the Special director on this account, but to my mind, it appears that as myself and Special director both were not prepared for premature chargesheet and chargesheeting of small fish alone, and perhaps I was also to be removed from the scene after Amod, it was all preparatory to that.

9. Besides, the Hawala case, my information goes that there were pressures from outside for my removal because of Krishnamurthy case and the LOC scam case of Assam in investigation of which, Shri Hiteshwar Saikia, Chief Minister, Assam is emerging as the kingpin. Since April '95, in Krishnamurthy case, director had a lurking feeling that I kept him in the dark in the operation to restrain VK from going to Washington on the night of 19/20th April '95. Kindly allow me Sir, to place it before you that there was absolutely no reason to keep you in the dark but there was no reason or occasion to inform you earlier than at the time I did. I had your mandate to file SLP then details are my business as JD. Since permission to file SLP was accorded by Government on your recommendation, the only possible conclusion was that Shri Krishnamurthy is to be prevented from going abroad as otherwise the entire exercise would be infructuous. Since morning on 19th April, we were trying to get the case fixed up for next morning which is done by the Chief Justice himself. We could not approach Supreme Court during day as copy of judgement became available to us from the High Court only at 4.30 p.m. on 19.4.95. We were told that for urgent hearings, the cases are taken to his residence by the Additional

Registrar General every evening. That day, perhaps there was no other case. Addl. Registrar General after hearing our case took the CBI team to the residence of the Chief Justice at about 8.30 p.m. but the Chief Justice left for dinner. They dispersed after deciding to meet him next morning at 8.00 a.m. and I was informed accordingly. Krishnamurthy had not told that he was leaving the same night, but at about 10 O'clock, the information came through his PA that he was leaving at 00.30 hrs, on 20.4.95 i.e. the same night. Amod K Kanth phoned me, we discussed that he will consult the Addl. Registrar General, if anything could be done to salvage the situation at that late hour as our efforts should be fully mobilised not to allow Shri Krishnamurthy to go abroad in the interest of our case. The other persons of staff were still in office. He collected them and went to the residence of Addl. Registrar General who asked them to come to the residence of the Chief Justice. Amod had now no occasion immediately to inform me that they had reached the residence of Chief Justice and till then, there was nothing that I could inform the director or the Special director. As they reached the residence of the Chief Justice, he also arrived and decided to convene the court there itself. Amod could neither leave the residence of Chief Justice and nor could he ring up from his residence to inform that the court had been convened. But still as a responsible officer, he managed to go to the telephone of the Chief Justice and informed me at 11.40 p.m. at night that the Hon'ble Chief Justice had decided to convene the court and I immediately informed the DCBI. I informed the director at the first and the earliest opportunity when anything worth mentioning occurred. As JD, I am responsible to control and to supervise the movements of my staff and inform my seniors only when there is something worth informing. If it had any political fallout, that is not a circumstance which I will take into account. If some politicians in power or out of power or anybody else gets angry, that is a non issue so far as I am concerned as a professional who goes only by facts and truth. To me, any mixture even of tact, in truth, deflects the truth from straightforwardness. You have given me a crime for investigation and I am a collector of facts. I collect facts in the rightful, legal and truthful way, to whomsoever it may hurt is no concern or consideration with me and in this case, I did not falter in informing you or I did not keep you in dark deliberately or otherwise nor did Amod. He informed me at the first available opportunity and same did I. If for travelling the path of truth, I am sent back to state or repatriated from centre or sent out from CBI, I am least bothered, as I have seen 23 transfers in 12 years and every time, I was transferred because of the principled stand that I took and it applies this time also.

10. Case of Krishnamurthy is a big scam by itself and its dimensions are very large and so are the pressures. Government of India have not allowed us investigations in Japan and Switzerland from where the kickbacks originated and were channelised through banks. Though, request for permission to issue L.R. was sent on 14.5.93, the permission has not come till today despite lapse of over 27 months. Earlier we used to apply to court for issue of L.R. under the law, and at the same time request G.O.I. to issue declaration of reciprocity, which was fairly a routine matter, but pursuant to Krishnamurthy's case, as my information goes, executive instructions curbing the law were

issued by G.O.I. and we have consequently been restrained by Policy Division Circular No. 21/44/89-PD dated 17th August, 1994 from filing request in the court unless G.O.I. permit us to move such application under section 166 A Cr.pc. It all speaks of the great influence and pressure Shri Krishnamurthy commands and exercises. As DCBI is aware, his influence and intervention did not stop at this. He could successfully dictate us through his contacts in government to file a lame duck Affidavit in the High Court where his application was heard on 18.4.95. it was on this point that we had arguments before filing the affidavit and again on 18.4.95, when his petition was allowed and he was permitted to go abroad.

11. Compromising a little here or there is perhaps more pragmatic in the prevailing circumstances where a civil servant feels himself helpless, but people perceive us as an agency comparable to FBI. We are supposed to investigate crime in high places. If we get bogged down for whatever reason, it does us discredit. While investigating the corruption in high places, our subjects normally have to be high ranking politicians and officers, if we start bending the law for them or interpreting differently, my conscience does not accept it. Will nobody or no agency in this country look into the corruption by high and mighty?

12. However, there may be some lapse or error, as a human being, which did happen once, and which I acknowledged immediately before you when I was late by a few hours in informing the disclosures of SK Jain. I was convinced of his disclosures on the night of 12.3.95 only, when I assigned the work of final compilation late at night, but it was just a slip that I did not inform about the disclosures then. The next

morning at about 10.30 a.m. in your office when I informed, you naturally told me that I should have informed earlier, perhaps you would have liked to talk to Jains. Whereas my lapse remains, but God is kind that on that day, we got remand to police custody of SK Jain extended by one day, which gave ample opportunity for yourself or Special director to have interrogated him. It salvaged the situation so far as the case is concerned or delay in information is concerned, but I agree that my lapse remains, though it was purely bona fide and only a chance slip.

13. I have the feeling that because of various pressures mine and AK Kanth's straightforwardness in both these cases, i.e. interrogation of SK Jain and recording of his statement and our role in reconsideration of Krishnamurthy case for proceeding abroad are not palatable at Government level. No individual is indispensable but I think the term of AK Kanth could have been extended as is normally being done in CBI. To my knowledge, no reference was made to Government at all which is a fair routine in CBI and for which in case of Amod his willingness to stay and my comments were asked for in February, but the situation changed in March and changed drastically in April. He was removed first and it was clear to me that I also had very limited time as JD.AC(HQ). I have no regret in being changed as I could not have been a party in leaving out the big and the influential while chargesheeting the small even if that is the interpretation we take of Supreme Court order.

14. The worst malady that ails our nation is the corruption and that too corruption at high places by high and mighty. Hawala case is a classic example where as per the accounts, we have so far, about Rs. 80 crores

were generated through kickbacks in which big people right up to the Prime Minister were involved. If we now concentrate only on minor functionaries, are we not aiding and abetting corruption? Catching Jains is the starting point only. There is no confusion that corruption occurred because of these high functionaries, Jains are only the peddlers who could do nothing if the authorities did not conspire and abet. Since nation has reposed its destiny in their hands and entrusted investigation of betrayal by them to us, to my mind we would be betraying our nation if we do not concentrate on big people. I strove for complete investigation into the power sector, which is draining this country. As kickbacks may be 3 to 10%, of the project cost, but up-valuation is anything between 40 to 100% of the basic and real project cost. It is in this context that I sent a report on Chamera Project to you where against an estimated cost of Rs. 1393 crores in 1992, the negotiations for allotment are on for Rs. 3300 to 3600 crores i.e. @ Rs. 12 crores per MW whereas in the world over rate of only around Rs. 6 crores per MW is considered reasonable for Hydro Electric Projects. Even if this figure were to be Rs. 2000 crores for 300 MW Chamera Project, should we not look into it when Rs. 1000 to Rs. 1500 crores of the nation are being squandered for kickbacks of Rs. 100 crores. This is the part which I was proposing to investigate and present a clear picture irrespective of the fact that who comes in. Certainly, some members of Union Cabinet both the present and past would come in and evidence against some of them was being uncovered. It does not matter if the name of former PM or the present PM figured or figured in a big way. As a professional, charged with the duty of collection of facts, I would not hesitate even if a big name comes in. Once we chargesheet the small, even if we do not intend to close the case, we would be forced to close the same, as happened in Dharmendra Deo Mishra's case and as per my information efforts are afoot in Assam LOC Scandal as the line has reached the Assam CM.

15. I am a low profile civil servant who seeks no publicity. But so far as the right action is concerned, I try to be absolutely straight and that is what I did during my stay as JD.AC (HQ) for 15 months and will continue to strive.

Yours sincerely,

Sd/-

(BR LALL)

Shri K Vijaya Rama Rao,

Director CBI

CGO Complex

New Delhi.

A copy is forwarded to Shri NN Singh, Special director (A) CBI.

Sd/-

(B.R. Lall)

Chapter - III

Pressures in Investigation, Particularly in the CBI

As against the claims made by the ministers during the discussions on the Bhopal Gas Tragedy that the CBI is a free and an autonomous agency, the insiders know that it is a fully and under command agency and the pressures in CBI are a day to day affair and almost universal in the cases against the high and the mighty. Verbal pressures are general and almost invariable in dealing with every big case and every big person, but even the written communications are not so rare as one from outside could think of or believe. The presumption is that nobody from the CBI will speak out as the rules against the same are so tight and also one risks his career, besides the accused will be able to take undue advantage of any controversy as in criminal law he has only to raise a suspicion and that is sufficient to throw away a cast iron case. In his book *Inside CBI* Joginder Singh clearly states about political pressures, "no serving civil servant will ever admit to its existence." There may be some mad exceptions like me who while in service would not only admit but would also protest and not carry out the illegal command. However, in general it is correct and these compulsions are exploited to the utmost extent.

The government servants do not go public and also normally they do not question as an average officer feels protected when such orders are received from above and particularly when such orders are received in writing. He normally carries out the written orders without even protesting or pointing out the irregularity or the illegality on the presumption that it is the responsibility of the person who gave such order. However he is mistaken as under the law the primary responsibility is on the person who performs the illegal task. The responsibility of the person who gives such orders is that of an abetter and can be punished only if the principal (the person who executes the orders) is punished. Only a few nonconformists make it a point to write back. While coming to CBI, I had visualised a different picture of its officers who were capable to take action against the high and mighty, but I was dismayed and when repeated efforts failed, I wrote the article titled "How to Make CBI a Free Agency" in the press that appears as Appendix to the previous chapter. I clearly brought out the pressures in the working of CBI.

The question was raised by many people, in the context of my contention in Bhopal Gas Tragedy over the various TV channels about the written missive received from the MEA that raised the entire furore and focussed public attention on the issue. Eyebrows were raised that the Government could not have sent the missive in writing as it does not appeal to reason. The person, who signs it, will be exposing himself to action. That issue now stands finally settled with the CBI confirming that it holds the same communication. The critics may be right that it may not be a general practice, but at the same time in actual practice it is not that unusual as well, for the same reason that they do not expect anyone to go public. I may cite an illustration of series of communications that were received in the case of an IAS officer Dharmender Dev Mishra of 1969 batch of UP cadre who was very well connected politically. After reading that account, one would realise that anything could be expected to be sent even in writing.

Two cases of corruption were on record against him in the CBI in 1994, in branches under my charge. A communication was received from the Government of India to close both these cases. We expressed our inability and replied accordingly. Then a demi-official (personal) letter was received from the then Cabinet Secretary Zafar Saiffullah to the address of the Director commanding the CBI to close both these cases. He was informed that one of the cases had been chargesheeted and was pending trial in the court and the other had been referred to the Government for prosecution sanction, so nothing could be done. After a few rounds of correspondence, the Cabinet Secretary finally wrote back demi-officially to the Director stating that Shri PV Narasimha Rao, the Prime Minister of India, had personally desired that the first case be withdrawn from the court and the second be closed as the Government was not according the prosecution sanction. It may be stated here for the benefit of a lay reader that, howsoever strong the evidence may be, no case of corruption under the Prevention of Corruption Act can be chargesheeted and sent to the court for trial without the permission from the appointing authority of the accused under Section 19 of the Act. Prosecution sanction thus is a prerequisite for filing any chargesheet. Further the appointing authority has absolute discretion to accord or to refuse such sanction that too without assigning any reasons as it is a question of personal satisfaction of such authority. Returning to Dharmender Dev Mishra case file, the worst feature was the last sentence of the DO letter that commanded the CBI that no more communications be sent on the subject and the matter be treated as closed.

What more can anyone write or what can be the greater pressure in writing than this that too from the PM himself? If such a written communication blatantly loaded with pressure can be received, the communication in question from the MEA is the most innocent, ordinary and routine in comparison. But look at the strength of the CBI and its officers that even this communication about Dharmender Dev Mishra that was personal from the PM, was not obeyed. I ordered to forward the same chargesheet to the court only replacing the word “Chargesheet” with the words “Withdrawal Report” at the top. The body contained exactly the same evidence as the chargesheet filed earlier. At the end of this so-called withdrawal report, instead of stating that the “chargesheet was being forwarded for judicial adjudication” it was mentioned that “in view of the orders from the PM, the CBI had no option but to forward the withdrawal report.” A copy of the letter from the Cabinet Secretary was also enclosed with the so-called withdrawal report, with the request that “the judiciary may like to take its own view.”

It was expected that the court would not agree with the withdrawal report as the judiciary was independent and need not fall in line with the illegal orders of the Government, whereas, we in CBI were slaves to the Government in power and could not go beyond the specific orders, even if verbal, whereas in this case the orders were in writing and specific that too from the highest authority in the land. Actually we had gone much beyond the accepted working norms. I could not think of any better alternative to oppose this illegality. Of course, I did not inform the Director and took it all on myself. I am not exactly aware of what happened at the end as I had to leave CBI before long, but so long as I was there, I am aware that the so called withdrawal report was not accepted by the exclusive CBI court at Dehradun. I violated in all essence the specific written orders of the PM. As suggested by Moily should I have gone public having filed this withdrawal report that no court worth its salt could accept? In how many cases can one go public? Incidentally by going public at that stage would have brought lots of publicity, if I were seeking that as alleged blindly by Veerappa Moily and Joginder Singh.

The Law Minister Moily talked of upholding the truth and shouting against the assumed pressure at that time rather after my retirement and is quoted in the media having also said "After retirement, people can give many statements. It is an irresponsible statement. This is not done at all. After retirement, people become martyrs by making such statements." Moily is ignorant of the fact that during tenure in service one is not supposed to interact with press or public. He himself is an advocate who should appreciate that making things public at that stage is sure to help the accused in the investigation and later trial of the criminal case. As a committed professional, how can one be so irresponsible to go public at that stage and damage the case? However I made all the possible protests against every pressure, in writing and verbally in various meetings and conferences very regularly and in many cases of such pressures, the issues were not directly even concerned with me personally. In my DO letter dated 1.8.95 (Appendix - II), to Rama Rao, the then director, I have clearly brought out not one but many such issues in a number of cases. Subsequently in my DO letter No 296 of 18.10.1996 (Appendix - III), addressed to the then Director CBI Joginder Singh, I have drawn his attention to his high handedness, his use of tools of discipline as tools of coercion, punishment and pressure to secure the desired results in investigations in various cases like Bihar Fodder scam, telephone tapping case and subsequently I accused him of interfering in JMM (Jharkhand Mukti Morcha) and other cases. On his trailing and meeting the former PM, Narasimha Rao, who was now our accused in many cases, I also had advised Joginder Singh in the internal meetings of CBI not to meet the accused persons, irrespective of their rank and status at the present or in the past, as that was against the CBI culture. No wonder that later on he was reprimanded by the Supreme Court for having called on the former PM who was our accused at that time. Further, in at least two of the above cases he was asked by two different High Courts to disassociate and his subordinate officers were asked to report directly to the courts. In view of above, were my protests and refusal to obey the pressures not enough while in service, when one is enclosed in the iron cage of discipline? Having protested so much and having written in press, the article "How to make CBI a Free agency" at tremendous risk to my job, can the Law Minister add anything else that anybody could have done? If he can give any tips, the crusaders of future will be able to take advantage.

On this occasion, I may tell the minister that I never yielded to any pressures either from the departmental bosses or from political bosses in my police career spanning over 37 long years. Disagreements, struggles and transfers were a day to day affair and the process commenced from the training days at Mt. Abu from exposing some small bungling there and the chain continued till the end. No wonder, for most of the time I normally remained on the so-called peripheral jobs, but even there the pressures were not missing. In my initial years as a junior officer I recall when pressurised, I had to write to the big boss, "...BR Lall does not take illegal orders from God, IG is only a human being." I felt sorry also as the IG himself was very honest personally and a well meaning person and whatever such order he had to pass was under pressure and belief that all these were in the interest and benefits of others so that they could cooperate for building efficiency and the welfare of the force. Knowing all this, still I could not condone the compulsion of my own big boss, who was considered the ultimate, a demigod in those days, in service matters. How at this stage of seniority I am bothered about anyone, who transgresses the path of truth and law, howsoever high and mighty he could have been? I am sorry I sound a little arrogant, though in fact it is only plain speaking that has become necessary in view of the minister's remarks.

In Hawala case, I had asked permission to investigate completely including search at their premises, amongst others, of the ruling Prime Minister. This is a matter of record on CBI files. Moily may see the same and if he has any regard for probity in public life, he should tender an apology to people of India for misleading them and to me personally for his unbridled misplaced outbursts against me on TV on 8th and 9th June 2010.

Incidentally, the professionals came out in the worst colours as Joginder Singh also stated in the same interview as referred to earlier "CBI is not an independent investigating agency. It is like any other department of the Government like PWD or Health and cannot do anything on its own." He goes on to say "CBI is comparable to a man who has to seek Government permission even for going to the toilet?

Contrast these above remarks with his attitude and remarks when he himself was the Director CBI. In November 1996 I had raised exactly the same questions of pressures and the same sentiments, in the three-day CBI conference. Apart from raising it in the conference I had earlier been raising the same very questions at all conceivable forums, meetings, conferences, on files as this was the burning question for me and for CBI that would assume relevance in all the situations. This conference was a three-day affair and this question cropped up for all the three days time and again with me in the lead every time. I had raised the fundamental question of pressures in CBI working, in great details that have been briefly summarised in the minutes of the conference as follows:

a) "The public had faith in CBI investigations in cases of small fries, the problem starts when it deals with cases against the political bigwigs.

b) in such cases, it was not in the psyche of the officers to go beyond a particular point. The general feeling is that after a particular point/limit, they should seek further instructions from Government and act accordingly.

c) To improve things he (BR Lall) suggested constitution of a (independent/autonomous) board vested with wide powers, including appointment of director, to supervise the work of CBI. This would remove the impression that the director of CBI is identified with the government."

Finally, these issues cropped up before the Prime Minister Deve Gowda, when he came to address the conference. In the conference comprising of 280 delegates from CBI, States and PSUs Joginder Singh as Director had consistently mounted severe criticism on me for raising the question of pressures on CBI while investigating the people at high places and repeatedly he took the stand that there were absolutely no pressures on CBI under him. To quote him "...that there were political pressures on CBI under me, is all a campaign to malign the CBI". The Home Secretary in his keynote address (as per page 36 of conference minutes) also quoted Joginder Singh "The director mentioned in passing that now we are quite autonomous." It is obvious that he wanted to convey that just with his taking over as director, all pressures had dissipated and CBI was absolutely on its own. But moot point is that how come in his opinion, now the CBI has fallen to the great depths as he has recounted now despite the subsequent Supreme Court judgment giving fixed tenure to the Director of CBI. Moreover how can he deny existence of pressures when he was Director of CBI and I was pressing the same point again and again and the then Home Secretary had also made an independent observation. Should Joginder Singh state at random even absolutely contradictory matters suited to the occasion without regard to the veracity of what he speaks? It was for raising such issues at the conference that I was prematurely repatriated from CBI within a month of the conclusion of the conference. Joginder Singh as Director of CBI pressurised the officers so much so that two High Courts independently had to ask him not to touch the files in those cases, but he was allergic to the word truth and any talk of pressures on CBI as he was part of the same establishment but now his language and sentiment has changed, a complete about turn, that does not behove a professional.

On 21 November in the conference itself, there was running argument between him and me for almost four hours as he would not allow any discussion on the subject of fighting corruption at high places and I wanted it to be discussed as this was the most important issue. He went to the extent of ruling "No discussions, as all discussions lead to confusion." Issue was partly resolved when the then Home Secretary, who was playing the host at the lunch on behalf of the Home Minister, found the conference stuck at the same issue from 11 a.m. when he left after delivering his keynote address in the morning and till the afternoon at 14:00 hrs as well, when he returned for the lunch. He took exception to the stand taken by the director as that amounted to very negation of the idea of a conference. Though I could push my way to be heard but it was enough to remove me from the CBI in the next four weeks. *Economic Times* of 30th December 1996 carried the lead editorial on this conference and my removal under the title "Revoke Transfer Order." An excerpt from the same is reproduced below and a copy of the editorial is attached as Appendix - IV.

"He dared to speak the truth and was shunted out of his job. The CBI Joint director BR Lall, at the annual meeting of the CBI and state anti-corruption officers held in November in New Delhi, merely pointed out what is a very common, and serious, problem faced by investigating agencies today.

That politicians involved in corruption cases interfere with the work of investigating agencies, hampering their progress. A few days later he was transferred out of the CBI for raising this topic at a meeting, which was supposed to discuss precisely these issues.... In fact the annual meeting of the CBI and state level anti-corruption officers would have been a farce if this important issue...were not discussed.... If the transfer order is not revoked, no cop would dare act against politicians he finds guilty in the course of his investigations.... Instead of nabbing the guilty, all he will do is to protect the politicians; because that is the only way he can protect his job. What is worse is that instead of taking action against politicians who interfere, Prime Minister HD Deve Gowda, reportedly asked him the reason for his discontent, as if there is need for another reason." What a prophetic analysis by the newspaper as CBI has been sliding downhill faster ever since the push downwards given by Joginder Singh.

Joginder Singh is now speaking the same language for which he severely criticised and took me to task at that stage when he was in power. Is he now not maligning the CBI or is it late realisation that how wrong and hypocritical he was. One wonders whether these contradictory statements suited for the occasion have any significance at all. I narrated all these in details in my book "*Who Owns CBI—The Naked Truth*" in an exclusive chapter titled "JUNGLE RAJ IN CBI."

Even now people in power are using pressure tactics so that no one speaks a word against their perceived line or interest for that the Hon'bles may have to resort to intimidation, threat or sidetrack what is true and correct. An ordinary person chooses to remain quiet instead of coming out and facing avoidable unnecessary travails and questions.

Can one imagine that so many Hon'bles, behaving like mafia dons, pounced upon me without regard to and without even ascertaining the truth? In such political and economic atmosphere of the country charged with such behaviour, scams, dishonesty and deceit, it is culpable to be truthful. Where truth has become a crime in our system, Moily is right in accusing me of being culpable.

Interference or pressures are the fundamental issues in investigation both in the states and in the CBI. It is a matter of common knowledge that in India all the decisions, including investigations whatever be the issue, are taken in the light of political interests of the party in power in a feudal style without any regard to the facts of the case or the national interests and the bureaucracy is ready or constrained to implement the same. Civil servants do not question even the patently illegal, unethical and the dishonest orders once they know that the same have emanated from or have backing of the powers who matter. Just to illustrate I recount a few actual incidents that would be the eye opener.

BANGLADESHIS SETTLING IN DELHI

In 1988 I had come to Delhi from Shillong to attend a high level conference on Police Community relations hosted by Delhi Police in Vigyan Bhawan. I came to Delhi a few days earlier to attend to other issues in the ministry related to the academy that I was commanding in the North East at that time. During my stay at Delhi, I authentically learnt from the Liason Officer Om Prakash of Delhi Police deputed with me that Bangladeshis were being issued ration cards at the spot within hours of their reporting. Police were also registering them, unofficially though, in order to keep a check on their anticipated criminal activities and Om Prakash himself was on that duty before being deputed with me. As they had no employment, the immediate conclusion was that they will live on proceeds from crime. Recording their particulars along with their fingerprints acted as a check on their criminal activities. Police personnel from state CID, charged with the work of registration, were mortally afraid of being exposed. I delved rather deeper as I had seen the consequences of Bangladeshi immigration in the North East where I had already served and lived for four years by then. By then about four lac such persons had been issued ration cards and also registered by the police in Delhi on the banks of river Yamuna where they initially settled as space was available there.

I raised this question in the conference in one of the sessions that was titled "Police at Crossroads." I stated the dilemma police face very often in their working and the Delhi police were facing a very serious one at that time. I was told informally that if the Delhi police raised this issue, they will immediately attract the ire of the authorities under whose orders the ration cards were being issued. Secondly they ran the risk of being termed as anti-minority as such allegations come handy from our political circles as has recently happened in terrorist cases like the Batla House case ignoring that the Bangladeshis are foreigners and have no place in India, under the law or the constitution. On the other hand if they do not raise the issue, they are failing in their lawful duty and their accountability to the nation. I sought guidance from the August House in general, and the distinguished panellists in particular as to what should Delhi police do under such circumstances.

I was intrigued that when I raised this issue in the question-answer session at the end of the presentations by the panellists, a senior police officer on the dais tried to brush the matter aside arguing that the issue had political overtones, so it should not be discussed in a professional get-together like that. Nobody raised a voice to the contrary and the issue was treated as closed conveniently. At this I protested arguing that if a murder were committed by a politician or if a politician were murdered, there would be political overtones either way, but there is also commission of substantive crime as well. Shall we, as police professionals, refuse to investigate? However my voice, though not feeble, but still remained a cry in the wilderness and the great professionals on the dais consisting of luminaries from the police, administration, media, academics all silently acquiesced to the accepted norm of golden silence. Conscience of all others was perhaps conveniently clear that if the police brass itself was not enthusiastic, why should they bother.

Such is the mental slavery that if the people in power are not likely to relish or appreciate, the police will not take cognizance of such a fact, of whatsoever importance it may be to the society or the nation. Besides police, administration was perhaps more obliging by issuing ration cards at an unheard of speed.

ATROCITIES ON WOMEN FROM UTTARAKHAND

The other bizarre incident of the feudal functioning and functioning under pressure and how people down the line are held responsible and people at high places go scot-free and how the whole administration arranges to protect the high and mighty even if the wrongs committed may be under their orders? This instance is from my CBI days from the state of UP arising out of agitation for formation of a separate state of Uttarakhand. On 1st October 1994, men and women from the hills were travelling to Delhi to organise a march, a demonstration and a *dharna* at Delhi on 2nd October to press their demand for carving out a separate hill state. Both the State as also the Central Government were opposed to the idea of the *march* and the *dharna.* During the day their vehicles moved smoothly on various routes through the plains of UP leading to Delhi, but in the evening hundreds of their buses were stopped, at Rampur Tiraha near Muzaffarnagar on their main route, from proceeding further. The traffic was held up for no rhyme and reason choking the road for 40 to 50 kms. At night there was mass rape of women and the protesting men were beaten and fired upon. At the time of rape the SP and the DC were both standing at the roadside clearly within the hearing range of the shrill cries of these scores of women in that otherwise dead silence. These high dignitaries were, perhaps under some orders, from some powers who mattered, not to listen to the wails and cries of the helpless women and naturally they did not and could not listen.

The case was investigated by the CBI. I came on the scene in this case in August next year when chargesheet was prepared. In the chargesheet the branch proposed to put up 245 persons from the rank of constable to inspectors and one DSP to stand trial. On the civil side also the highest officer was one SDM only. The DC and SP were perhaps recommended for some lighter action. After considering the evidence and that who ordered the action on the ground, I dropped the names of 240 subordinates retaining the SP, DC, SDMs and the DSPs, but adding criminal liability against all of them. I also added the names of IG, DIG and the Divisional Commissioner for criminal action. Informally their defence was that they were under orders from above, but for obvious reason, as usual in such cases, none will admit it officially. In the whole process of investigation that I viewed at the time of chargesheet, I could see an invisible hand directing all these activities including the carnage at night. The law officers opined that the evidence against the Divisional Commissioner was not enough for being prosecuted, so the departmental action for major punishment was recommended against him and the six other senior officers including the IG, the DIG, the SP, the DC, the SDM and the DSP, were all chargesheeted after securing approval from the director and the charges were dropped against 240 men as that will only have prolonged the trial and ensured that enough confusion was created to scuttle and bury the case and allow all to walk out that too at the initial stages.

Had the law enforcement been independent and not under pressure, the DC and the SP will not have silently witnessed all those atrocities on the people and much less on the women.

CM ORDERS ARBITRARY ARREST OF DLF CHIEF

The following incident will show how pressures for illegal acts are exercised by the people in power to settle personal scores. In 1969-70 I was posted as ASP Rohtak district in Haryana. The SP went on leave and I held the charge of the district in his absence. One morning as I reached my office I got a call from the DC informing that verbal order of CM were conveyed to him for passing on to me to put Raghvender Singh, chief of the prominent building company DLF, under arrest. I asked him for what reason as we did not have any case against him. The DC informed that the CM secretariat wanted to talk to me but since I did not have a telephone at my residence, so they asked the DC to convey the same. In those days the ASP was not given any telephone or transport. In the absence of SP I had access to his telephone while in office as I occupied his room, but did not have the facility at my house. He suggested that I could enquire from the CM Secretariat.

Instead of enquiring from the CM Secretariat that would have been a verbal enquiry, I sent a wireless message to CID in police HQ informing the order of the CM, along with the fact that we did not have any case against him and as such we did not need him. I asked for informing what for was he to be arrested? No reply was received and the matter died down, but a little later a senior officer from CID HQ visiting the district took me to task for sending such a written message. His advice was that once such orders from CM are conveyed, police officers themselves are supposed to look for and search excuses for arrest. He also tried to frighten me by saying that it was with great effort and persuasion that I could be saved from the fury of the CM. It was correct that Bansi Lal, the then CM was a terror and all the officers from all the services were mortally scared of his wrath and no one asked him any questions. Later I learnt that it was my message in writing that basically prevented any action not only against the DLF chief but against me as well. But imagine the pressures, for misuse, on the investigating agencies that are exerted for unthinkable issues. Later on they only have to defend themselves against whatever illegality they might have committed under the so-called orders for which they have to manufacture a second lot of stories and alibis.

Here I may emphasise on one lesson that I learnt from this incident that helped me lifelong. That reduce the free frank and honest views into writing as soon as possible as I did in case of the CM's order to effect the illegal arrest. No wonder, in subsequent years I had disagreements, by and large, with all my bosses on point of principle at one stage or the other. However experience with Mr PA Rosha was altogether different. He was Police Chief of Haryana between July 1977 and February 1979, a very turbulent post emergency period. I was his Chief Staff Officer as AIG. We were always on the same wavelength of upholding the truth and to work strictly as per the law of the land in complete disregard to any other consideration. Once in a very serious matter instead of expressing my views in writing I took the file to him to discuss the consequences as the Government had already given an inkling and pressure from that side was acute and my thinking on the issue did not fall in line with that. I told him that I had brought the file for discussion in advance so that it may not embarrass him once the contrary opinion was on file. That was the only time Mr Rosha took me to task and regretted that "It was not like Baldev (as he used to address me with my first name)." He commanded me to examine it in the light of facts and law on the file and then only discuss if I felt the need and never think what the boss wants or thinks. I took back the file and recorded my views. He agreed with my views and further recorded strong support and then went on to discuss with the CM who could not overrule the written word and approved the action as proposed by us. The problem with our bureaucracy is that normally first they discuss the inconvenient matters with the powers and then they get bound to record convenient notes.

In my whole career this was the single such instance, but the lesson was deeply imprinted on my mind and there was never any looking back. It is for this reason that in CBI also I always brought all the facts on the file without batting an eyelid even if it may be inconvenient to or disliked by the high and mighty

On the other side, immediately after 3-4 days of the incident I received a call from DLF chief Raghvender Singh profusely thanking me and offering a plot in his latest colony that he was developing at Gurgaon, but I declined the offer straight away telling him that since all that was a part of my official work, so I will never accept or even purchase any plot in any colony developed by the DLF under him. I have honoured my words till this day despite the fact that Gurgaon, my home town, has emerged as the development hub of the DLF.

COLLECTION OF TRUCKS

One fine morning in 1970 when I was still an ASP and was in-charge of district traffic, the SP called me and introduced to one Satram Dass Batra (Malik), MLA Kalanaur and told to place 35 trucks at his disposal at Kalanaur for various villages in his constituency to bring people for CM's meeting where Bansi Lal, the Chief Minister was to usher him into the Congress party. Batra was a Jan Sangh (now BJP) MLA and was scheduled to join the Congress on the appointed day for which the trucks were asked to be provided as cost free transport to ferry people. The list in *Urdu* on the letterhead of Batra contained the names of 23 villages to which 35 trucks were to be deputed. The CM had telephoned the SP to supply the trucks. In routine I placed the letter in my pocket and asked if it constituted our lawful duty. The SP sent me away and never bothered but the trucks were collected as he directly asked the ASI Traffic to do so. I recorded the facts on the back of the communication on the letterhead of Batra. This document along with my observations at its back are reproduced below:

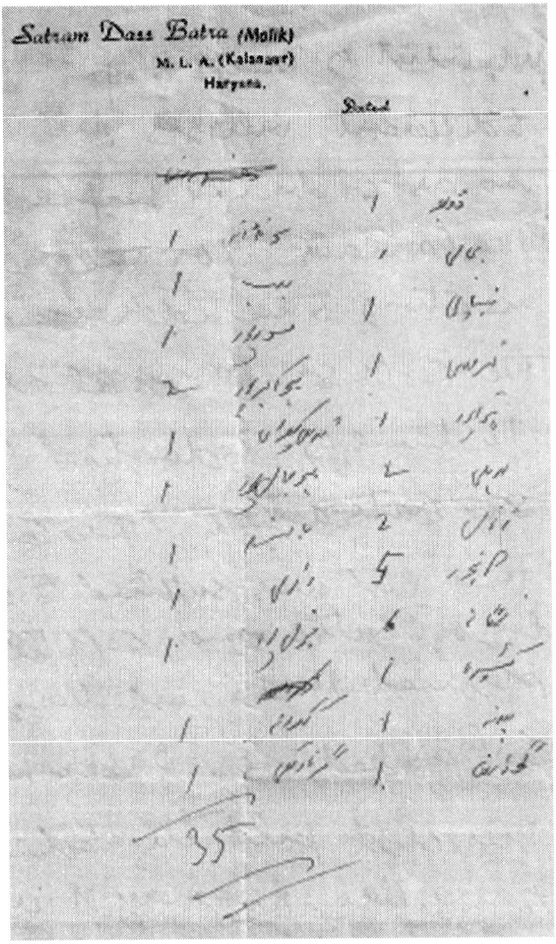

Satram Dass Batra (Malik)
M. L. A. (Kalanaur)
Haryana.

Dated

Villagewise list of Trucks to be sent
to different villages on 14-11-70
so as to bring people to
Kalanaur for the Public
meeting to be addressed by
the C.M. Sh. Bansi Lal at
the time of induction of
Sh. Batra into New Congress.
This list was supplied to S.P.
by Sh. Batra and C.M. tele-
phoned that this must be done
S.P. asked me. I after pocketing
this chit politely declined
to oblige. Anyway it was
done by the Traffic Asstt.

[illegible]
15-11-70.

It was per chance that I had not been geared up into the routine. It was a fair routine that whenever there was a political or a state function, the SP will be asked to supply the trucks and the DC to arrange the crowds. The crowds would then be taken to the place of function. I also learnt that if the opposite party wanted to organise a function, with their own men and material, the administration and the police would put in every possible spoke to make it impossible to hold such a function effectively. Their men would be dragged out and arrested on one pretext or the other, their vehicles would be stopped and impounded and for which they might have paid or they might belong to them. Besides, the transport services would be suspended and some time even the trains would be cancelled. Either way the might of the state was galvanized to make the function of the government or that of the party in power a success and to employ all methods and tricks to ensure that any function by the opposition ended in failure. That was the mindset of the police force, the district SP and the District Magistrate. I wondered if we were living in a state where the Constitution was supreme and ensure level playing field to everyone. Incidentally the core is still the same but the fear of being covered by camera and later the TV screen has made some difference.

Despite putting up stiff resistance as ASP, it appears that my mindset was also taken over as I also fell into the same rut and as District SP at Narnaul in January 1971; I also collected the trucks the same way when Mrs Indira Gandhi, the Prime Minister was to inaugurate the Lift Canal at Ghikara village in Dadri Sub-Division of my District. The only saving grace was that it was a state function and not a party function. The mindset had so overtaken that I forgot all the sense of propriety, Constitutionality, legality and morality that I had upheld when the SP Rohtak had desired me to collect Trucks for Batra only sometime back.

I realized the full consequences in 1977 as District SP Jind. Those are the days of emergency and functions of CM, the Defence Minister (whose visits were rather frequent as he belonged to Haryana) and the State Ministers were held by dozens in a month in every district. By that time the routine was so set that SP was hardly bothered. The local MLA would notify the local SHO and he will supply the number of trucks as demanded. In the first week of February 1977, I was appalled when the president of the local Truck Union approached me to excuse them from requisitioning their trucks so frequently that too without providing even the diesel to them and moreover he pressed that for 22 days in January the trucks were on fatigue duty of the government or the party in power. He rued how could they carry on their business if for 22 days the trucks were with Police and they were only required to fill up the tanks with diesel. Unbelieving, I asked him for details and was surprised that he was correct as the trucks would be collected 2 days before the appointed date. Next day these would be handed over to the Tehsildar or his representative i.e. Patwari, Kanungo, BDO or the Gram Sewak. The third day it will perform its duty, fourth day it will collect its documents, the fifth day the driver and the cleaner would have rest and visit their village and it was only the sixth day that the truck could be available for the business. Four functions meant 22 days and during January there were four such functions when the VIP or the so-called VIP had visited the District.

Earlier, we were not taking the documents in our possession but the trucks after dropping the people at the venue of the function would run away. To bind them, their documents were taken in Police custody so that the trucks dropped the people back home after the function. This had become necessary after experience of one such function as some trucks had left and the available trucks had to be overloaded. One such truck met with an accident killing one or two people. Situation did not deteriorate as the driver of the truck belonged to the same village as the passengers and they also happened to be relatives. They did not want to register the case. I got a daily diary report registered and informed the Police Headquarters accordingly. It was necessary to inform as deaths had occurred. I was summoned to the Headquarters with full facts of the matter and was pulled up for not registering a criminal case against the driver. I was armed with statement of the people that there was no negligence on the part of the driver and that it was a case of pure accident but still I was directed to register a criminal case against the poor driver and then cancel it or send it untraced after a month or two if nobody stood up to the contrary. I was intrigued at the panicky reaction of the nervous Police Headquarters that did not want to shoulder any responsibility. It was a lesson in instituting a false and fictitious case which did not exist. However, I had no alternative but to register the case on the statement of a Police Head constable and then to report it as untraced. But the hypocrisy of our working under pressures caused revulsion in me. I was already under orders of transfer in first week of February. I assured Sh Bhagwan Dass, the president of the Truck Union that in my future charge as district SP or range DIG or as Police Chief, I will never allow such a practice, but alas! I was never posted to district or range and I worked as Police Chief for barely 50 days in order to conduct elections impartially.

Thanks to the Election Commission that close to elections such things have stopped. It was Seshan who as Chief Election Commissioner had initiated such processes. Further, thanks to Indian Democracy and Indian politicians that elections take place many times in five years with the result that most of the time watchful eye of the Election Commission prevents this patent misuse of state authority and the violation of law. However, for the functions in between, the same practices continue even now. How can an administration and a police force so subservient have a mindset and conscience of its own?

POLICE COMPULSION TO PERPETUATE BONDED LABOUR

Two months after joining the District in March-end in 1969 I was posted to understudy one urban Police Station for one month. I worked with the Station Writer, called Dewanji or the Moharrir to learn about Police Station records. I also used to observe the dealings by the SHO, though he invariably avoided taking me to any crime scene and also did not transact any meaningful business in my presence. I however, made it a point to informally interact with everyone who visited the Police Station for any work or who was brought to the Police Station for questioning. That gave me insight into when should I force myself on the unwilling SHO to the scene of crime and also asked him to conduct the particular business in my presence. One day as I entered the Police Station and started conversing with the people sitting for questioning, I found that a whole family of brick casters from Rajasthan had been brought to the Police Station. As usual they denied having committed any wrong, and even the persistent questioning could not get anything. On my enquiry from the SHO what for were they sitting in the Police Station, he informed me that one brick-kiln owner had handed them over as they were running away from the kiln. That confirmed the story as told by the labour but with the only difference that the kiln owner had verbally made certain allegations. In case the labour agreed to return, these allegations were not to be pursued but if they insisted on going away these accusations had to be acted upon and they were to be arrested for stealing and misappropriating money of the kiln owner. I again checked with the labour that had altogether a different story to tell. The labour confided that they had not been allowed to stir out of the kiln for the last two years. On the paper they had been paid much more but in reality they had to purchase all the rations and other requirements through a shop run by the kiln owner himself, at very high prices. As a result their entire earnings were taken away and hardly they were left with any money to go to their village in Rajasthan. They felt helpless in fighting the kiln owner who was a very influential person.

When confronted with their version, the SHO confessed that the labour was right. The kiln owner was very respectable and very close to the CM and that the SHO could not go against him. I ordered the SHO to let the labour go as they were the citizens of the free country and could not be restrained like that and much less by the arm of law. The SHO educated me that all the kilns were running on such exploitation and that without Police help no brick kiln could be run even for a day. He also warned me that by releasing them I would be incurring the displeasure of the owner and even SP would not take kindly as he (brick kiln owner) was the man of the CM. My conscience was intact and unimpaired. I asked him to let them go on my responsibility and also told him that if he had recorded any report in the daily diary, I would record a further report and absolve him of any responsibility that he may fear. Very satisfied I left for lunch but when I came back the family was again sitting there. The SHO told me that the owner had brought them back and he could be coming any moment. When I was talking to the SHO the owner appeared at the scene. I had a detailed discussion and tried to convince him that it was illegal and not part of Police functioning but he was adamant. When I announced my intention to let them go he threatened me with dire consequences. I escorted the labour to the Bus stand, made them board the bus to Rajasthan side and deputed a head constable to ensure that the brick owner does not catch them again. The head constable was to escort them to Rajasthan.

Within an hour I got a call from the SP who wanted to see me immediately. The SHO was gloating that he had already warned me. As I entered the office of the SP, the kiln owner was already sitting there. The SP politely requested him to wait in the waiting room and asked me about the event. When I explained him the chain of event and what had happened and how I was upholding the legal and human rights of the poor citizens, he smiled at me and called back the owner. The SP then sweetly talked to him in my presence and told him that the young new ASP was doing his legal duty. That the ASP was in the Police Station for a month only and he should cooperate. The brick owner left at this, though not satisfied.

This made a deep impact on my mind that how Police were a party in violating the human rights and perpetuation of the bonded labour. They did not gain anything except perhaps the favours of brick Kilnwalas who were rich people and quite influential. Most of the Kilnwalas were listed as helpers of the Police and provided the much needed transport for investigation and otherwise for use of police and others whom police were constrained to oblige including the officers from judiciary. There were quite a few categories of business people whom I found helping the Police in any and every situation. Not only with the wherewithal but also with cash whenever it was needed for their functioning or meeting private needs or adversities created by the exigencies of services for whatever reasons. Apart from brick kiln owners the liquor shops walas, the goldsmiths, the transporters and a few others fell in this category. Bad elements among Police either extorted or sought help from non-respectables like the Sattawalas or brothel keepers or opium traders. Money or help from such people was considered as immoral but not from the above respectable categories.

It is this mindset of slavish mentality that becomes part of life of not only the police officers, but of the whole administrative set up and the higher the level the more intense is the sense of slavery. Basically it is the good discipline that is ingrained in the policemen, but the reality of power structure accompanied with this sense of discipline, turns them robots. Conscience does provide the protective shield against the pressures, but when one has to give in to the pressures repeatedly, the pressures blunt the conscience.

That is a dangerous state of affairs. There is urgent need to free investigation if the rule of law, the cornerstone of any democracy, is to be upheld.

I can cite any number of examples and burden the book with documents that I still hold back. Initially I had thought of including another half a dozen cases and communications, but then I thought that these examples are enough to bring home the point and the reader need not be forced heavy dose of self righteousness, though some of it was unavoidable to drive home the crucial point. In next chapter I deal with the CVC, how effective the institution is. The CVC was intended by the Supreme Court to free the CBI from external pressures, to safeguard the functional autonomy of the CBI and watch from the angle of fighting corruption, but my experience unfortunately shows that it is an ineffective organisation that by its inaction, lethargy and lack of will encourages malpractices, in curbing corruption. CVC has fallen short of our requirements and some more potent organisation needs be provided in place.

Appendix – III

Central Bureau of Investigation

D.O. No. 296/JD(N)/CBI/96
GOVERNMENT OF INDIA
C.G.O. COMPLEX. BLOCK NO.3
LODHI ROAD
NEW DELHI-110003
Dated October 18, 1996

B. R. LALL
JOINT DIRECTOR (NORTH)

Dear Shri Singh,

When you took over as director/CBI, you had advocated and promised complete transparency in the functioning of CBI, but unfortunately it is the hush-hush atmosphere, which is prevailing. There is no certainty about anything. The deep thought which should precede any action in this sensitive Organisation both in operation and in administrative fields has given place to sudden impulsive orders. The system of transfer of charges instead of presenting transparency is leading to dark alleys.

On 7.10.96, there was a usual weekly meeting, which lasted till past 12 noon. There was no mention about chopping off my charge, but in the afternoon sometime between 3 and 4 p.m., DIG, Chandigarh rang me up why I was being divested of the charge of Chandigarh. Since I had no official information despite the fact that I was with director till 12 O'clock, I declined any knowledge, which shocked the DIG. At the tea table when I mentioned this to my colleagues they were also surprised at the manner.

I tried hard to figure out the possible reasons. I could not guess any except that (believing that working in CBI should be free of fear and be transparent) I have been commenting freely on certain decisions, which to my mind have been against the CBI culture of truthfulness and have been affecting vitally the organisation and its reputation. I also made comments on Biswas affairs on the narration of Shri RC Sharma, which was unfortunately in your absence otherwise I would have commented on that in greater details there itself. When you re-entered the room, the meeting was dismissed as you had some immediate commitment in courts/ with AG.

Such hush-hush transfers are becoming a tool of punishment to the so-called inconvenient who work and speak truthfully. The mechanism is also designed as a pressure device for others to fall in line. If my transfer was a part of re-organisation, it should have been discussed or at least I should have been sounded in advance, I authentically came to know of it only on the 8th (AN) i.e. next day. When facts are suppressed rumours take over. Already lots of rumours are afloat. While promising transparency, why these hush-hush orders were made leading to rumours is not understood. Rumours or guesswork are detrimental to this sensitive Organisation.

There has to be some reason for every action and there must be some reason with you, but if that reason cannot be told, cannot be transparent, it naturally leads to the conclusion that there is something fishy.

Similar things have happened in case of the Special director when immediately on your taking over he was practically divested of all the work. Subsequently the telephone tapping case was given to him, which even a naïve would realise was only a cover up and the real intention was that DCBI wanted to sideline the Special director as his advice in some cases could have been a stumbling block. Similar is the impression that has gone down in CBI with two time transfers of Shri UN Biswas confining him to Patna only and stranding his family or taking him off from Patna altogether.

I have always followed the dictum that "act well thy part and there all the honour lies". But I find that the tinkering with the system, breaking it at will gives the impression down the line that director does not want straight forward functioning and those who do not fall in line, are being divested and harassed. My reputation actually gets a boost by such actions as I have established my reputation here during 2½ years and in state and Government of India during last 2½ decades, but if my organisation, which is so dear to me, suffers, it pains me. This unpredictable action, for which no reason or rationale has been shown takes the morale of CBI cadres down, which hurts me. I shall feel grateful if I could kindly be informed why this chopping off was done and why in a hush-hush manner without any transparency. I believe that I and whole of CBI openly is entitled to know that.

Yours sincerely,

Sd/

(B.R. Lall)

Shri Joginder Singh

Director, CBI

A copy is forwarded to Shri RC Sharma, Special director. I am sending this copy as I have made a mention of the name of my senior, so, I feel morally bound to endorse a copy.

Sd/

(B.R. Lall)

Appendix – IV

THE ECONOMIC TIMES

30 DECEMBER 1996 VOLUME 36 NO 257

Revoke transfer order

He dared to speak the truth and was shunted out of his job. The CBI joint director B R Lall, at the annual meeting of the CBI and state anti-corruption officers held in November in New Delhi, merely pointed out what is a very common, and serious, problem faced by investigating agencies today. That politicians involved in corruption cases interfere with the work of the investigating agencies, hampering their progress. A few days later he was transferred out of the CBI for raising this topic at a meeting which was supposed to discuss precisely these issues. What is worse is that instead of taking action against politicians who interfere, Prime Minister H D Deve Gowda, reportedly asked him the reason for his discontent, as if there is need for another reason. It is widely known that several cases under the CBI were not even properly investigated under the previous administration, like the St Kitts case and the Lakhubhai Pathak case, because of the alleged involvement of former prime minister Narasimha Rao. The Pathak case is over 11 years old and the St Kitts case more than eight year old. Political interference in the JMM and Bihar fodder scam is also well known. In fact, the annual meeting of the CBI and state level anti-corruption officers would have been a farce if this important issue was not discussed. Which is what it has turned out to be, looking at the reaction of the CBI director, Mr Joginder Singh to this issue.

Prime Minister Gowda should ask Joginder Singh to take back the transfer order. If the transfer order is not revoked, no cop would dare act against politicians he finds guilty in the course of his investigations. He would merely, as happens even now, bow under political pressures. Instead of nabbing the guilty, all he will do is protect the politicians, because that is the only way he can protect his job. We need more cops who have the courage to publicly reveal the names of politicians who put pressure on them. This is the only way to ensure fair and free investigations. Otherwise, it will be impossible to catch corruption at the political level.

Chapter - IV

How Independent and Effective is the CVC

I was sick of the Jungle Raj in the CBI as Joginder Singh, the Director, had plunged the agency deep into that mire. In 1997-98, I decided to expose him, but could not get any opportunity. Ultimately I decided to complain to CVC about his bunglings in CBI. Finally, on 1st January 1999 I addressed a DO letter (copy attached as Appendix - V) to N Vittal, the first CVC appointed under the statute, giving a brief account of the five selected cases, highlighting his negative role and the consequent injustices and the illegalities and requested the CVC to take action. At that time I was very much in service and that too in Government of India as against the chorus harped on me by Veerappa Moily and others that I am protesting after my retirement. I had offered all the assistance and further evidence, but the issues were not taken up. In the next two years I followed it with five DO reminders, all of them addressed personally to Vittal, the CVC. Besides addressing the DO letters I called on Vittal five times, i.e. once in between every such letter and impressed upon him to take action as otherwise the institution will not be able to stand on its feet and the injustice and indiscretions will continue. I am adding two such intervening letters dated

22nd August 2000 and 1st December 2000 as Appendices VI and VII. A reading of these three DO letters is self explanatory and clearly reveals how serious the charges against the former CBI director were?

However nothing happened in the two years since 1.1.99, except an interim reply that comments had been asked for from the CBI. I called on the CVC, for the last time, on 26th December 2000 and had frank discussion why he was not taking any action. I was intrigued at the unbelievable reaction of CVC who said "what can I do, the Government is not supporting me, the CBI does not care for my directions. Nobody is happy with me...." That day I clearly told him that he was not able to discharge his functions as CVC and was ineffective. I suggested to him that he was not in regular service. He was in a statutory tenure post after retirement and will do better service to the nation by resigning if he felt so helpless as he gave me to understand. He had no reply. I waited for some action by him, but not finding any in sight for the next six months, I wrote to him another DO letter dated 27th July 2001 (copy enclosed as Appendix - VIII), politely stating the same sentiment that I had talked to him, though not so politely on 26th December.

A reading of these letters and the above account shows how weak, helpless and ineffective is our institution of CVC as well. The way this institution is designed, it can never be effective and courageous. Till then it was a new institution ever since it was recreated under a statue, but by now it is over a decade old. However if we see its achievements, it is all next to nil. Besides the routine advice to departments in disciplinary cases, it has not brought any revolution in waging war against corruption, as it was expected to herald. The causes for this dismal performance lie in its constitution and the framework under which it functions.

The selection procedure of CVC by itself is defective. The CVC is the same bureaucrat placed in the different role of a watchdog over his own previous role. The process of appointment itself makes him beholden to the executive bosses. There is no reason why he should be neutral, but even if he tries to be, his mindset and the system he is placed in, prevent him as we have seen.

The selection of present CVC, Thomas to succeed Pratyush Sinha clearly proves the above hypothesis and has brought the issue into focus. Thomas has a registered case against him, pending over a decade on the allegations of corruption, along with the CM Kerala in the Palmolive Oil Import case. The case was duly substantiated in investigations and chargesheeted. The same is pending trial, for want of prosecution sanction, in a Kerala Court. If it were not for such a well connected officer like Thomas, the officer would have been under suspension. There could be no question of his having been empaneled as Additional Secretary and Secretary to Government of India. Further, for 8 to 9 months before moving to Satarkta Bhawan, he was Secretary Telecom with minister Raja who is facing the biggest ever scam of the country known as Spectrum 2G Scam. Pratyush Sinha, his predecessor had taken it up as a star case and the same is under active consideration. It is a matter of common sense and does not require any skill to conclude that he will not be able to function objectively, nor will he appear to be so. It has appeared in the media that these and such other issues were raised by Sushma Swaraj, leader of opposition in the Lok Sabha. She is an ex-officio member of the committee for selection of CVC. As per democratic norms and traditions in such matters in UK wherefrom we draw all our parliamentary traditions, the disagreement by the leader of opposition is treated as good as a veto as the office of the leader of opposition is treated as an institution by itself. If you have such an institution on the committee rather than an ordinary MP or an ordinary minister, you have to extend due respect to it so that the person representing such an institution can exercise effective check that will not be possible for the members of the ruling party. However if the leader of opposition can be overruled by the majority opinion, it can always outnumber the leader of opposition, then where is the big deal in having him or her on the committee. The entire exercise in this case is meaningless as the PM and the Home Minister will always be on one side and continuance of the leader of opposition will be of no use.

There is another side to it that the CVC so selected is aware that he has been favoured. It is irrespective of whatever personal merit he may have. He knows and realises that he is obliged to the Government and in particular to the PM and the HM and may be many more persons that operate from behind, who all made his selection possible in the face of such difficult situation. He will always behave like a slave to all these and the two, i.e. PM and HM in particular. Tomorrow when he selects the Director CBI and Director Enforcement, there is no question of his being independent. He will ensure that any candidate proposed by the Government will be selected by hook or by crook, as happened in his own case, even throwing away or circumventing the letter and the spirit of law, the principles laid down by the Apex Court in Vineet Narain case or more famously known as Jain Hawala case. It may involve bending or misinterpreting the rules or misuse of the discretion or even the patent *dadagiri*. Such a director of the CBI who is slave to another slave, will never be fair and impartial. It is also true of the Director Enforcement. With such infrastructure, it is futile to expect justice and fair play at the hands of the CBI and the Enforcement Directorate. Three institutions namely the CVC, the CBI and the Enforcement Directorate stand killed with a single master stroke. It is widely believed that his appointment is to cover-up the telecom scam. A section of the thinking population believes that following the great tradition of cover-up culture in our administration, the scandals that are breaking everyday in the context of the

Commonwealth Games, will also be hushed up. It is widely rumoured that the Government will assign the scams to the CBI after the report by the committee. The act of bringing in the committee, by itself, will allow a few months time to the accused persons to cover-up and destroy the evidence. Later the CBI will entrust these cases to a specially chosen officer who will scuttle all the scams and whitewash the whole affair. Such an officer may be picked up out of the existing lot or may be posted to the CBI from outside for the purpose. He will have the advantage of the blessings of a committed CVC so that nothing will be difficult. The veracity of this view will soon be tested, but in the present circumstances the people feel it is probable and possible.

Unfortunately, both the moral and the legal fibres are very weak in our country. If legal fibre were strong, the objections raised by the leader of opposition would have been respected rather than being overruled. If on the other hand the moral fibre were strong, first the Government would not have put up a name whose integrity was suspect. If at all such name did come up, that would have been dropped at the very first appearance of public/media criticism, but under no circumstances could the name continue to be under consideration, rather no one in Government would have dared to touch his name even with a barge pole once the objection was raised by the leader of opposition.

There is another aspect that for CVC the essential requirements are that he should be honourable and a person of integrity and morals. How could Thomas accept such an offer even if made, when he knew that a criminal case of corruption duly chargesheeted, was pending against him. Now the case has been fully discussed and dissected by the media and whole range of information in the case is in public domain. It is now very clear, that it was a case of corruption duly registered, investigated and chargesheeted.

Since Karunakaran, the then CM of Kerala is also an accused, the case has been tossing-up and oscillating depending upon which governments rules the State. It is a sad commentary on our system that the law is subordinate to politics. How can then we boast of rule of law which is the life blood for any democracy? But case of Thomas was referred for according prosecution sanction and has remained pending with Union Government for years. In between as per the accounts that have appeared in the media, the CVC gave him clearance following which he was promoted at least at two steps. The argument now given is that CVC did not find anything against him in this case. If case for prosecution sanction has been pending, how could such an inference be drawn. If these reports are correct, it makes the successive CVC, stand in the dock along with the Union Government as the Government are the authority for grant or refusal of prosecution sanction. They are also the authority to grant promotion. Why they did not look into his record. It raises a doubt if the opinion was procured form the CVC and projects CVC as a conspirator in the sordid drama.

This brings us to the further question that till such time the prosecution sanction is given, no court can take cognizance and as such no trial can commence. If for 7 years Thomas ensured that the Government slept over the issue, should Thomas be presumed as innocent. It is a foregone conclusion that all influential people manage such pendency and project themselves as victims later. As a matter of fact the provision for prosecution sanction by itself is bad in law and was perhaps created by the British to secure the loyalty of such people who would go astray but were useful for the continuance of the empire. This should have no place on statue book in free India. It is against all the legal cannons of jurisprudence and an enemy of the rule of law. It requires to be removed from the statute book, but if still it is to be retained, another proviso be added that the appointing authority should take decision and convey the same within 90 days of the receipt of the request and if it fails to convey within that stipulated period, the law should raise automatic presumption that the permission is granted.

Having managed the denial of prosecution sanction by keeping it pending they invoke the great judicial dictum “One is presumed to be innocent till proved guilty.”

Let us examine this issue in more details, for this has become a very contentious issue as the interpretation of the highly sacrosanct provisions has been moulded to suit the criminal requirements of all the corrupt in the Government that unless one is convicted of a charge and the conviction is maintained by the final court of appeal, he is not to be treated as guilty. The provision was in the context of not inflicting any punishment on any one unless he was proved guilty. It is a sound judicial principle that holds protection against premature curbing of individual liberty. Liberty is the basic fundamental right that can be curbed or curtailed only according to the due process of law. But appointment to a particular office is not a fundamental right and as such denial of any appointment does not amount to a punishment and as such does not attract the above provisions as that dictum has been laid down in context of punishment basically. On the other hand we require outstanding people with impeccable integrity in all the public offices and the requirements are much more stringent for the watchdog of the morals of others. Even a faint shade of suspicion about the integrity of a person should be enough to disqualify him from any post in the Government and much more so for such sensitive posts as CVC or the like. Incidentally in the UK from where we draw our constitution, even a suspicion is enough to compel one to resign from the constitutional offices. Such offices are held in trust and confidence, whereas, suspicion is the antithesis of both. Extending that very principle, no politician or bureaucrat or anyone else should be allowed to occupy any office under the Government, if he has ever come under suspicion and has not been fully cleared of the same. The principle, in this context, should be modified to read that 'if ever suspected, one will continue to be under suspicion till finally cleared completely.'

Why should people under suspicion rule us? There is no need for us to tolerate the tainted persons in these sacrosanct offices, as we require and deserve the fairest of the fair to lead us and not the pick of the scum who are under accusations or suspicions. If such a person continues to be in power, first he will block the evidence and break or even eliminate the witnesses and ward off the conviction by misuse of his office. It is for this reason that no accused person from the higher echelons of society has ever been convicted in any corruption related offence during last six decades. Second, this honourable criminal in high position would have wrought irreparable irreversible further damage before conviction, if at all that ever comes about. That is the rationale of the contemporary miserable state of affairs the country has sunk into.

It is argued by the political class that false accusations are often made against them by their rivals and if on mere suspicion one has to face ouster, no one will be able to function at all. For that the system of preliminary enquiry that has the approval of the Supreme Court, amply takes care. Under the criminal law, a criminal case has to be registered immediately as the information is brought to the notice of police and all enquiries have only to follow the registration. However, in corruption cases in view of the above problem, the Supreme Court in its judgment in Serajudin case from Madras, reported in AIR 1971 page 520, upheld holding the preliminary enquiry prior to the registration of the formal FIR. However they further laid down the principle that once the preliminary enquiry prima facie showed that some offence had been committed, proceedings in the enquiry should stop, a formal FIR be lodged immediately and investigations should be taken up under the Code of Criminal Procedure. Since then many more judgments have been received on the subject that take care of the problem. It automatically follows that if the preliminary verifications return him guilty, he should be eased out of the office and also debarred from fighting elections before even the commencement of the detailed investigations and till such time he is finally cleared. However still there is need to sort out the question of delays. The corruption cases against the politicians can be put on the fast track in the courts, so that they are not prejudiced from fighting elections.

It may be added here that there is need to do away with Section 26 CVC Act and Section 19 PC Act, so that the CBI and the CVC have the discretion to register a case as per their professional judgment. There should be no need or requirement of going to Government for various processes during investigation and trial, including filing of SLP, review petition or for engagement of special counsels.

Reverting to his case, it is more than clear that Thomas did not deserve even the consideration for selection to the post of CVC. It is however a different matter that the CVC Act does not stop him as the Act has no requirement of honesty or integrity for the post. As per the CVC Act, the Government also have committed no illegality or impropriety.

This crucial point legally goes in his favour that the CVC Act Sub-section 3(a and b) of Section 3 that prescribes the qualifications or the eligibility criterion for the CVC and the Vigilance Commissioners, does not talk of integrity or honesty as a requirement for the post of CVC and the VCs. Sub-section 3 of Section 3 of CVC Act is reproduced below:

Section 3(3): The Central Vigilance Commissioner and the Vigilance Commissioners shall be appointed from amongst the persons:

(a) Who have been or are in an All-India Service or in any civil service of the Union or in a civil post under the Union having knowledge and experience in the matters related to vigilance, policy making and administration including police administration; or

(b) Who have held office or are holding office in a corporation established by or under any Central Act or a Government company owned or controlled by the Central Government and persons who have expertise and experience in finance including insurance and banking, law, vigilance and investigations.

On the other hand there is rightly a specific provision of integrity in case of Director CBI and Director Enforcement in Sections 26 and 25 respectively of the same Act. The relevant provisions of the two sections are given below:

For Director CBI Section 26 reads: "...The committee shall recommend a panel of officers on the basis of seniority, integrity and experience in the investigation of anti-corruption cases...."

For Director Enforcement Section 25 reads: "...while making a recommendation, the committee shall take into consideration the integrity and the experience of the officers eligible for appointment...."

Does that mean that the CVC need not be a person of integrity and the Government as such have not bothered about the same?

However, the Supreme Court judgment in Vineet Narain case and the subsequent Law Commission report on the basis of which the CVC Act was enacted, expressly lay down the integrity requirement. One wonders if this provision was left out from the Act deliberately or it is just a lapse. If it is a lapse, it is terrible and needs to be corrected immediately. If, however it is deliberate, it is not only most reprehensible but also culpable.

Could the Union Government go to the extent of making a false statement regarding the pending case against Thomas? What a shame that the government should be compelled to stoop so low! There is no dearth of outstanding officers with certified integrity, then what is the compulsion to make such a person the watchdog for maintenance of standards, rule of law, honesty, integrity, ethics and morals in the country of which he himself appears to be bereft. If he himself had the sense of morality and self respect, Thomas would have declined the offer at least after having known the circumstances and in particular after the great hue and cry from the public.

But where is the morality or rule of law in any field in the system of our governance. Both have been casualties ever since the independence. The case of appointment of Thomas has further exposed the system as the way his case has been carried through and he has been picked up and installed. In perception of the layman, instead of appearing to be a watchdog, he prima facie appears to be a conspirator in the sordid drama of corruption being enacted in the country in the most naked fashion, or at least a collaborator that he will whitewash them and in turn the case against him will get scuttled by the Government that has the ultimate veto in every criminal case. The Governments have reserved to themselves the right of withdrawal of any case that too in public interest as this author observed in his book titled *Who Owns CBI : The Naked Truth* "...arguments of public interest can always be coined.... as if corruption is being continued in public interest or for the existence of public order or survival of this great nation, which by implication cannot survive without these corrupt and dishonest elements and without their corruption and dishonesty. It is a beautiful arrangement that persons in authority commit the crime of corruption...if investigations are conducted, they only direct the collection of facts, they only decide on prosecution and finally on withdrawal. Whatever serves them gets defined as public interest. In all this so-called public good, the country is looted, bled, drained and deprived."

That incidentally brings us to the system of post retirement employment in general that operates more as a spoils system. Rather than ensuring neutrality, taking straight decisions or inconvenient decisions in context of the powers that be, such appointments encourage favouritism and corruption. The common man feels that they must have obliged the powers during service or at least just before their retirement or must have promised directly or indirectly to protect their interests, otherwise why should they have been selected leaving out other scores of officers equally or even more competent. When there is no criterion or system of selection, the allegations do stick. It is well known that for any service, may be judiciary, administrative, technical or professional, there is no process for these constitutional high post-retirement jobs. Having been in service, we all have observed how the prospective aspirants start lobbying and wooing the powers during last phase of their service just before retirement. Some of the most honest officers do patently wrong things while at the threshold of retirement just to earn post retirement bonanza. In case of judiciary from time to time it keeps recurring in the media and becomes a talk in the Bar that the judge delivered a motivated judgment just before the retirement and lo and behold! soon he is rewarded with some job that may be on a Commission or a Tribunal. It has also been discussed in the media that for certain posts there are traditions that a judge occupying a particular position will take a particular job after retirement. This is a good tradition or arrangement as that obviates obligation to people in power, but when Justice RC Lahauti, the retired CJI was not posted to NHRC, it was a talk in the legal circles that he had refused to oblige the Government in his judgments so it was intended as a punishment or more appropriately, denial of reward. This is part of our feudal culture that requires loyalty to the persons in power rather than to the State. This is true of all irrespective of the political shade of the party as that makes no difference.

We need to evolve procedures for functioning of the State in all its aspects. The essence of democracy is the rule of law as against the arbitrary wish of the ruler who may be a king or a feudal lord or an elected leader or anyone else. For filling in the post retirement jobs, strict criterion need be laid down and followed in letter and spirit, though the efforts should be to bring most of such jobs into the fold of the serving officers. For instance in judiciary the age of retirement has been raised to 65, so more judges would be available. If there is still some requirement, raise it to 70 years. Besides more posts could be added to the cadres so that serving judges could be deputed on Commissions, etc. That incidentally would also obviate the avoidable unpleasant controversies like the one that arose in case of Gujarat arising out of Godhara incidents when motives were imputed to the judges as one judge was seen as a nominee of Narendra Modi, the CM and the other as a man from the camp of Lalu Yadav, the Railway Minister. Such allegations against the judges undermine public confidence in judiciary, which is laden with very dangerous trends. So long as serving judges cannot be provided, the centre should maintain a roaster of judges willing to serve on a Commission, Tribunal or any other job after their retirement and the person next on the roaster should be asked for sitting on or heading the panel. No selection or discretion be possible at this stage. Similar should be the case with the civil servants. They should also have similar roasters for particular jobs and the senior most on the panel be deputed for the job for which he is registered. That will free them from any extra constitutional loyalties. Though the ideal arrangement for civil servants, like judiciary, would be that in their final years who opt for such jobs, could go to these panels and retire from there. Whatever system is followed, it should be free from the sense of gratitude to anyone. Further, there should be a bar on taking any job either in Government or in private or doing business for 5 years after retirement for people holding such jobs. They should also be barred from taking up job as independent directors in the companies in corporate sector.

Coming back to the question of the CVC, even the above will not meet the requirements for the job. For the combine of the CBI and the CVC, we need a powerful organisation that can function on its own without any reference to Government in power. We need an umpire who can check the people in power on its own. After all, the corruption by the very definition is a crime committed by the people in Government, the public servants both amongst the politicians and the Government servants. A watchdog authority is required and the umpire, the referee or any other type of watchdog cannot be a part of the same set-up. As such the CBI and the CVC have to be independent of the executive and have to be high powered in order to pull their weight. That is necessary in our feudal mindset. I recall reaction from late Chander Shekhar, the former Prime Minister of India in the context of investigation of Hawala case. In that case under the orders of the Supreme Court in 1994, the CBI was asked to examine and record the statements of all the persons named in the Jain diaries in order to know their side prima facie. Chander Shekhar remarked that now ministers and the PMs will be examined by the pigmy thanedars. The contempt for the officers was clearly reflected from his feudal mindset. Basically the contempt was for the law that these CBI officers represented and enforced. To be effective under such circumstances, the institution has to be heavy weight by itself, but at the same time it has to be far more accountable, though to a different and independent set-up. In all the countries that have been able to come out of the muck of corruption and now rank high on scales of integrity, such institutions invariably exist. They take suo motto action for entire gamut from what to investigate, what to enquire, when to register the offence and what to chargesheet. That actually is an effective deterrent against corruption. If only such a body had existed in India, the numerous scams related to Commonwealth Games or the mega 2G Spectrum Scam would not have occurred nor would continuous all-pervasive corruption have plagued us and we will have been saved from the endless scams and scandals. In Bhopal Gas Tragedy case also, such a body would not have acted under any pressures. What we need is a high powered Independent Commission against Corruption as exists in Australia, Hong Kong, Malaysia and many other countries under the same name. Besides, similar independent institutions exist under various names in other countries. Whatever be the nomenclature, the essence lies in independence of action. In whole of the well meaning civilised world, every country has such an independent agency which functions absolutely free from Government.

There is another aspect to it that howsoever fair the agencies and the Government may be, but so long as these function under the control of the Government, these will remain vulnerable to the charge of partisan behaviour, irrespective of the party in power. The mutual blame game of the political parties is of no use to the people. They may square their accounts by taking turns in misusing and accusing, both rightly and wrongly, but either way the credit of the agencies suffers and that adds to the woes of the people. Free agencies may be against the political interests of all the political parties but are certainly in public and national interest.

Coming to the details, every country has evolved its own model and we can also have our own one. The provision for the commission could be made in the Constitution itself or under a statute. The Supreme Court in its judgment dated 18th December 1997, in the Jain Hawala case, envisaged the CVC on somewhat similar lines while developing the subject, but missed the mark when it came to its structure on the ground. The proposed commission should be a pluralistic body whereas CVC is only a three-member body. Further, it is packed with all the freshly retired former bureaucrats, who in the opinion of the former Cabinet Secretary TSR Subramaniam carry with them the mindset of slavery which is the very antithesis of independent action. Incidentally, such bureaucrats cannot so easily forget their masters and also the lobbying that they had put in to get the coveted post. Such a commission or body for enforcing integrity on this nation is not a good alternative and will not serve the purpose. Second, a committee selects the CVC, who in turn has to be beholden to the selectors who are the members of the executive, whereas the members of the commission as visualised by this author, should be thrown up by the system automatically and there should be no element of selection so that the members are not obliged to anyone. Third, in the CVC system, the selection of the Director of CBI and the other senior officers is again predominantly with the members of the executive only. The commission will combine all the functions of the Government in relation to all the institutions engaged in fight against corruption including the CBI, the Enforcement Directorate, investigation wing of the income tax, etc. All the powers whether of permission as at present under Section 26 CVC

Act or prosecution sanction under Section 19 of the Prevention of Corruption Act 1988, will vest in the Commission, i.e. all other powers and discretion, now being exercised by the Government and the CVC would become the prerogative of the Commission that could have about a dozen members as follows:

CHAIRMAN

i. Last retired Chief Justice of India

MEMBERS

ii. Last retired Comptroller and Auditor General of India.

iii. Last retired Chairman of Chief of Staff Committee (defence)

iv. Last retired Director of CBI

v. CVC (serving)

vi. Last retired Chairman, University Grants Commission.

vii. Last retired Governor, Reserve Bank of India.

viii. Last retired Cabinet Secretary.

ix. Last retired Speaker of the Lok Sabha or Deputy Chairman of Rajya Sabha, who must have finally retired from active politics (One of the two by rotation).

x. Last retired Chief of Central Board of Excise & Customs or the Central Board of Direct Taxes (One of the two by rotation).

xi. Serving Director of CBI as the Member-Secretary.

In case the last retiree as proposed above refuses to come on the board, the person who retired from the same position earlier to him shall be invited to join as the Chairman/ Member as the case may be.

The Commission would thus have 11 members with a quorum of seven but the presence of the Chairman and the Secretary should be mandatory. The Commission must meet once a month or more often as per the requirement.

After serving a term on the Commission they would be debarred from taking up any job, consultancy, independent directorship, arbitration or advisory role either in the Government or in private.

Chances of pressurizing this high powered multi-member Commission would be next to nil as they have nothing else to look forth after retiring from this Commission. All the members are high dignitaries retired from diverse fields and such positions of responsibility that collectively they will neither commit any indiscretion themselves nor allow any being committed. Since they would represent a number of disciplines, the CBI/ED would be able to get specialised guidance in various spheres, which may enable them to conduct investigations much better. At the same time someone or the other will understand the technicalities of various cases in details. That will exercise a healthy check and prevent any officer from going astray.

All the operational and the administrative powers would be vested in this Commission, including grant of prosecution sanction, selection of director and other officers including the disciplinary powers. The Commission could relegate such powers as it may think fit to the Director of CBI and the chiefs of all other agencies under its control.

After the approval of the Commission, the Secretary (Director) would send the annual report of the bureau to the Parliament and could also appear in person before the Parliament whenever desired by the Speaker and place before or explain to the sovereign body any particular documents or issues.

The Union Government will have a right to refer any case for investigation by the Commission and the Commission shall be bound to register the same and investigate as per the law in the same manner as if it were a case registered on its own. It will send no report during investigation to the Government. However the Government will be informed of the final outcome.

Had this system been in existence, the CBI would not have yielded, among others, in the Bhopal Gas case. The same is further corroborated in the context of CVC by the recent instances of Adarsh Society Scam of Mumbai, the CWG scam, and mother of all the scams, i.e. the 2G spectrum scandal of telecommunication. Once such big scams have been committed and the information is in public domain, the CBI as also the CVC should take cognizance *suo motto* and take up enquiry/investigation as the facts demand. In the CWG (Commonwealth Games) and the 2G Spectrum cases there was further advantage that even the formal reports of no less than the auditing giant, the CAG, have been available. Further, so much information is available with the media that has been disseminated along with the original documents that as per the Supreme Court judgment referred to above, the preliminary enquiry should have been dispensed with as there is enough reason to believe prima facie that the offences have been committed. If only our institutions were independent, they would have taken up the investigations immediately on their own, but all these under command institutions, with their subaltern mindset, as their top brass is under obligation to the Government of the day, cannot be expected to deliver. No wonder they fail to rise and measure up to their task and we as nation are on the same cover-up track by appointing a committee that is against the Apex Court ruling, will only waste valuable time, delay investigation and help the criminals to cover their tracks and destroy as much evidence as they can.

However the fact remains that no institution in the field at present can stand on its own. Reverting back to my complaint to the CVC against the former CBI Director Joginder Singh, if the CVC had any self esteem, at the first opportunity, it would have taken action on my complaint, but no one has contacted me till this day. If any enquiry was to be initiated, I as complainant would have been the first to be contacted. Alternately if the allegations in the complaint were not true, the CVC should have proceeded against me as I was very much in service in 1999 and continued till 2004. It was possible even after my retirement. I was subject to the departmental and service discipline, but nobody would dare when my defence was the TRUTH itself.

It also settles the starting point and answers Moily and other critics that it is not after retirement that I am making noises, but always I was like that, but the only change is that it was internal fight then, but now it has come into the open. In the CBI itself, I was first shifted from the zone dealing with cases of people in high places, then subsequently one-third of my new charge, i.e. DIG Chandigarh was taken away. Further, I was threatened with shifting of my HQ from Delhi to Lucknow, throwing thereby my family life out of gear and posing threat to the education of my children, who would have lost one to two years and all this without any purpose or gain to the institution. Besides my confidential report was categorized as average thereby downgrading it steeply from outstanding, which is not permitted by rules even unless it is conveyed to the officer. Internal fight is always more difficult, but away from public eye. Incidentally this is not the end to what I protested and recorded, but much more and in many cases to which the CBI files bear the witness. However I still have in my possession a few more such documents, but I do not want to strain the reader with repetition of the similar sentiments, though in different cases.

Appendix – V

बी.आर. लाल, भा.पु.से.
निदेशक (अनुसधान एवं विकास)
B.R. Lall, I.P.S.
Director (R & D)

Tel. : (O) 4361726
(R) 4671633

पुलिस अनुसंधान एवम् विकास ब्यूरो
ब्लाक ११, तल नं. ४,
केन्द्रीय कार्यालय परिसर
लोधी रोड
नई दिल्ली–११०००३.

Bureau of Police Research and Development
Ministry of Home Affairs
Block No. 11, 4th Floor, C.G.O. Complex
Lodhi Road
New Delhi-110003 Dt. 1.1.1999

Dear Shri Villal,

I felt reassured by your determined statement, to achieve a society with zero level of corruption, at the Book release ceremony of Shri Joginder Singh's book on 29.12.1998 at Press Club. Prima facie it appears to be a tall order but it is very much within the means, the reach, the capacities and capabilities of this country to achieve it. The next morning, I read in the press that the efforts of Shri Joginder Singh have been appreciated at the ceremony in the Animal Husbandry case of Bihar. I have known Shri Joginder Singh till 31.12.1996 when I was Jt. Director with him during his tenure in CBI and have known his functioning and style, his political overtones and many faces. He has no regard for professional integrity/ honesty as illustrated by a few cases which I am citing as examples.

AFZAL PURKAR CASE OF MAHARASHTRA

Shri Joginder Singh immediately after taking over as Director CBI ordered that this case (also known as Bombay Port Trust Case) should be charge sheeted by the month end. The orders were not for finalizing the investigation but for charge sheeting. The pressure was inbuilt in the order itself and coming from the departmental chief, was worse than the political pressure. The Joint Director pleaded some difficulties as the investigation was yet to progress but everything was overruled and the whole of CBI Bombay office was put on this case. My Additional Legal Advisor (ALA) was deputed to Bombay with clear directions to ensure that the case is chargesheeted. He spent perhaps two weeks or more there and the case was built up, but by month end, the orders came from Shri Joginder Singh that the case is to be dismantled and not to be chargesheeted. Services of my ALA were again taken for a few days more. Whether Shri Joginder Singh was doing so under political pressure or on his own, he knows better, but surely the action was neither honest nor straight. Seeing the political dimensions of the case, it appears that he bowed to the political pressure not once but twice, first while ordering the chargesheet and second while ordering the dismantling of the same. Only one of these actions could have been right, and that should have been thrown up in the process of investigation itself rather than being directed either way.

AHD CASE OF BIHAR

This is the much talked about case which Shri Joginder Singh is supposed to have chargesheeted in the face of opposition from the then Prime Minister, Shri Gujral. I have no reason to know what transpired between him and Shri Gujral but the background, before Shri Gujral took over and the role played by Shri Joginder Singh is well known. During the very first week Shri Singh took over, tussle started between him and the Jt. Director (East), Dr. U.N. Biswas. Shri Joginder Singh did not want this case to be investigated whereas Shri Biswas wanted to reach the conclusive end. It was widely talked about in CBI and Shri Biswas confided in me also. Things came to a flash point in the last week of September, 1996 when the report was to be filed in Patna High Court and Shri Joginder Singh wanted all references to Mr. Laloo Yadav to be deleted whereas Shri Biswas had mentioned 4 point evidence against Shri Yadav. He showed me a copy of his report. Shri Joginder Singh deleted it completely and wanted Shri Biswas to file a report approved by him to which Mr. Biswas did not agree. The task was ultimately given to Shri R.C. Sharma, the then Special Director to produce a final draft, which should only mention the name of Shri Laloo Yadav, avoiding details of evidence. The only mention should be that his name has also figured. Shri Sharma prepared a draft accordingly, but Shri Joginder Singh while approving the final draft deleted all the references to Shri Laloo Yadav and submitted a different sealed report in the Patna High Court through, of course, Shri Biswas on 30.9.1996. When the court read the contents of the report and sought confirmation and clarification from Shri Biswas, who was present in the court itself, then only he came to know that the Director had not been honest and straight. He then told the High Court that it was not as per his report. That is where the controversy arose and appeared in the press and the High Court took an unprecedented step to bar Director CBI from looking into this case and asked that all the records should directly come to the Court from JD and not through Director. Within the CBI, Shri Joginder Singh was made persona-non-grata so far as AHD case was concerned.

What followed has amply appeared in the press and this situation continued till last week of March or possibly early April. As per Press reports, when the political equation at the Centre changed and his mentor, the then Prime Minister Shri Deve Gowda, parted company with Shri Laloo Yadav. At this stage, it was clear that his place would be taken by somebody else as Director CBI, sudden change came in him and as a calculated strategic move, not motivated by consideration of justice or truthfulness, he ordered the chargesheet. Though this was the right decision, but it was itself out of malafide and ill motive, just for his own survival or as counter political pressure. All this somersaulting should be available in CBI records or if Shri R.C. Sharma and Shri Biswas are asked about.

J.M.M. CASE

In the JMM case also he interfered with the investigation so much so that he asked the then S.P. Arun Sinha to change certain notings, but the latter did not oblige. He hounded out the SPs concerned with the JMM Case. Shri Arun Sinha was posted to Silchar as part of harassing techniques as Shri Joginder Singh used transfer as a tool of punishment and as a mechanism designed as a pressure device for people to fall in line. There are many such persons who fell prey to his machinations. Shri Vivek Johri, the other S.P., in this very case, opted for repatriation after abut two years of joining the CBI. Though I know from my personal knowledge that he is a very brilliant and straight forward officer but if he cannot be effective in the right path, he will either fight for justice or will opt out. At that time, fight would have proved counter productive because politically Shri Joginder Singh was very well entrenched. Shri Johri had no option but to get out. But immediately the Delhi High Court came to their rescue and brought the entire team back and asked them to report directly to the High Court and not to Shri Joginder Singh or any other authority subordinate to Shri Singh. It thus took away this case also from the purview of Shri Joginder Singh. This is the second case in which the Director CBI was made persona-non-grata by two different Courts as they felt that he was not allowing proper investigation and was rather interfering the path of truthful handling. In other words, the High Court found that his approach was not honest.

UREA SCAM CASE

It was another big scam where again proper investigations were prevented by Shri Joginder Singh. Shri Joginder Singh is quoted by the Hindu as saying "If the percentage of loot was reasonable, I would not have written about it. It was suffocating to do with wrong doings and humiliations from the powers that be". If it is so, why he gagged investigation in most of the important cases and in this case transferred Shri R.M. Singh, DIG when the investigation in this case was at peak and at a crucial juncture. It is correct that earlier Shri Vijaya Rama Rao had not allowed investigation when it came to the family members of Shri P.V. Narasimha Rao, the former Prime Minister and had recalled R.M. Singh from Hyderabad but Shri Joginder Singh went hammer and long after him and transferred him on the plea that he had completed 17 to 18 years in Delhi. It is correct that R.M. Singh had been in Delhi for long but the kingpin of the investigation in between an important case is not changed in CBI. In all fairness he could have waited for a month particularly when that is a case of 100% bungling as all monies disappeared without receiving even a kg. urea. He was immediately relieved and was not given time even to have a cup of tea with his staff. Even if the argument of Shri Singh is granted, why other officers like Arun Sinha, Vivek Johri etc. were moved out when they had not even completed the term and Vivek Johari had spent only about two years in CBI. The pattern is clear. Whosoever was forthright, was inconvenient, transfer was the tool to punish him and to remove him from the investigation of that case so that the evidence could be collected in a pre-determined manner.

He played political games all through his tenure. It is also learnt reliably that while taking lift in the car of Shri Narasimha Rao in first week of August 1996 just after taking over the CBI, he was executing the political mission of assuring him of all protection and help in the cases being investigated against him by the CBI.

He propounded the principle of transferring those who had done a particular period at Delhi but after transferring the first inconvenient lot, he did not touch other officers. Then he came straight to constables. He repatriated about 250 of them. The intentions were again not straight. He filled up all these vacancies through one central recruitment at Jalandhar in Punjab against the established practice of CBI that SPs recruit constables locally as and when vacancy arises. On the contrary, he created vacancies and made recruitment making it amply clear that this was an action to oblige his own kith and kin. Otherwise there was no question of one point recruitment. It inflicted lots of difficulties and problems on all the constables, who fought upto Supreme Court against their repatriation. Some of them had to be retained but others, terribly suffered. In all actions, there is always a purpose and a scheme and the reasons are coined accordingly.

PUNJAB AND SIND BANK CASE

The same trend of obliging people or falling under pressure is visible in the Punjab & Sind Bank case, which was registered in CBI. Even at the time of registration of the case, it was known that if there was some case, it was against the Chairman of the Bank, but under orders of Shri Joginder Singh it was made out against one General Manager who had opposed the grant of loan in question tooth and nail on the file. This man came to me crying and showed me his own noting which I confirmed from CBI files as I was in CBI at that time but the officers dealing with this case showed helplessness as they were under pressure from the Director. You will kindly appreciate that one can fight political pressures but it is extremely difficult to fight the pressures of departmental bosses. The GM was to be arrested but he had taken

Anticipatory Bail. But since the Chairman happened to be a friend of the Director, CBI, pressure was exerted on investigating team. Now after years of investigation, the position of Mr. N.S. Gujral, the GM of Punjab & Sind Bank has been vindicated. He asked me a question "Can these two years of mind boggling tension be given back to me. Can the loss of prestige that I and my family suffered be given back to me?" He also told that he was on the verge of promotion, which was stopped only because of this case. Well, I had no answer. But the CBI records can prove the patent malafide, sense of dishonesty and the pressures exercised in the case.

Sir, I have tried to illustrate the functioning of Shri Joginder Singh, by citing the above cases. For his personal interests or of those in whom he was interested, all through he conceded to pressures and also pressurized his subordinates. Pressures, political or others, must have come on him but the head of an organization has to absorb those pressures without passing them on to his subordinates and there is nothing so great about it. I had come to the book release ceremony to confront Shri Joginder Singh with the above instances where not only he buckled under pressures but passed it on to his subordinates. Those circumstances, I think, are not yet in your knowledge. On seeing yourself presiding over the function, I decided to withdraw as the Press could have interpreted it unkindly. As responsible civil servant and more so as former CBI officer having worked with him during his tenure as Director CBI, I feel it my duty to bring this to the knowledge of highest supervisory authority of CBI in the country. You may kindly like to verify the facts from the CBI records in these and other cases and appreciate the role of Shri Joginder Singh as Director in that light and may like to take, if deemed fit, some corrective steps.

With regards

Yours sincerely,

(B.R. Lal)

Shri N. Vittal
Chief Vigilance Commissioner
Jaisalmer House
Mansingh House
New Delhi

Appendix – VI

B.R. Lall, IPS

D.O. No.
Director General of Police &
Chairman-cum-Managing Director,
Haryana Police Housing Corpn.

Dated 22nd August, 2000

Dear

You may kindly recall that I had brought to your kind notice vide my DO letter No.DIR(R&D)/I/MISC./99 dated 1.1.1999 certain instances about the functioning of Shri Joginder Singh as Director, CBI and that how he brought politics, the hush hush atmosphere laden with fear as opposed to Truth and transparency which impart honesty, integrity and straightforwardness to investigations. I had expected immediate response, but on not receiving any, I addressed another DO letter of even number on 16.2.1999, volunteering to assist and also to give some more information. It was also intended as a reminder, I have not received any response despite the passage of nearly twenty months.

As a complainant in this case, in a transparent system, I am entitled to know what happened to my complaint. My fight in CBI for which I was jettisoned out of Hawala Case by Shri Vijai Rama Rao and subsequently out of CBI itself by Shri Joginder Singh was on the basic principles that we do not take any action against the higher ups, that we become paralytic the moment we are faced with investigation or prosecution against the big i.e. any action against corruption at high places. Am I to presume that, in the same strain, mighty Joginder Singh is also not to be touched even by the CVC for whatever may be brought to his notice?

Incidentally, repeatedly I had brought to the notice of Shri K.V.Rama Rao and again to the notice of Shri Joginder Singh when he was Director regarding what was going on in Chamera Project that negotiations were being held at Rs.3500 crores for a 300 MW Project about which I made a formal report to Sh. Rao but no action was taken as the general administrative culture in our administration as also in CBI is to spare the big and the influential. Initially I verbally brought this to the notice of Sh. Joginder Singh in early August 1996 but there were occasions for formal communication and I wrote to him twice in this context, once vide my letter dated 2.9.96 which was addressed to Shri N.N.Singh, Special Director regarding certain other things but in para 8 on page 4 I have made a mention about this serious Source Information Report and I also enclosed a copy of the report. There was also an occasion while examining petition No.660/96 filed in Jabbalpur High Court submitted by Shri D.N.Naik of Hindustan Steel Works Construction Limited, Calcutta, a Government of India undertaking opposing allotment of works worth Rs.640 crores to TYAZHAPROM EXPORES (TPE) a Russian firm. While examining various issues, the Chamera Project became relevant and I again made a mention of the same at para 5 of my note dated 22.8.96 and enclosed a copy of the SIR, still no action was taken. Fortunately the CMD of NHPC was changed. I discussed the matter with the new incumbent Shri Narsimhan in details & requested him not to be a party for allotment of the project. The project remained unalloted till 1998 when fresh tenders were called and work alloted at Rs.1684 crores in place of Rs.3500 crores in April, 1999. The relevant question is why Sh. Joginder Singh did not look into. He rather termed it as a “wild goose chase” though now the chase has brought fruit & country has been saved Rs.1800 crores despite the escalations that might have taken place during the four intervening years. Even now it needs to be looked into why rates of Rs.12 crores per MW, which were beyond the wildest imagination of anyone, were entertained at all for negotiations. Shri Joginder Singh by now had become desperate on my insistance on taking fight against corruption to high places which he never wanted incidentally. I am enclosing a copy each of the noting on petition 660/96, SIR dated 29.5.95 in case of Chamera Project-II, my DO letter dated 2.9.96 and shall solicit an early response. For your ready reference I am enclosing copy each of my DO letter dated 1.1.1999 and 16.2.1999 as well.

I am prepared to come to Delhi to assist yourself whenever required.

Yours sincerely,

sd/-

(B.R. Lall)

Shri N.Vittal,

Chief Vigilance Commissioner,

Central Vigilance Commission,

Satarkta Bhawan,

INA, New Delhi-23.

Appendix – VII

Tel. No.561838 (O)
565265 (R)
D. O. No. 6989/PS/CMD/HPHC

B.R. Lall, IPS

Director General of Police (H)Chairman
cum Managing Director
Haryana Police Housing Corporation Ltc
211, Sector 6, Panchkula

Dated the 1st December, 2000

Dear

I had approached you with details of specific cases in which Mr. Joginder Singh as Director CBI had not functioned in a straight forward and honest manner. I wrote to you on 1.1.1999 but till date no action has been taken. First time I heard from your office is vide No.99/HMA/14 dated 17.10.2000 addressed to Director CBI. From this communication I conclude that from your office the same was referred in September, 1999 only i.e. almost 8/9 months after I approached you. You will kindly recall that I had called on you twice followed up with reminders and also made offer to assist in case any clarifications were required. Then in August, 2000 I addressed you another DO letter in which I raised certain questions of basic importance in big projects and brought out how country was being bled and drained and how no preventive steps were being taken against corruption at high places. I was actually encouraged by your press statements of 1998 onwards and it was for that reason that I was expecting some immediate response accompanied by some immediate actions but I am sorry to point out that a specific complaint from quite a senior officer who had himself witnessed these bunglings by Shri Joginder Singh the then Director, CBI, and had stood up against the same, has been accorded such cold reception by yourself and by your office. How could an ordinary complainant get the wheels of justice into motion, if I at my level have failed?

I would request you kindly to guide me how to get justice for the ordinary people of this impoverished nation as in whole affair I have nothing personal and during my CBI stay also I had nothing personal. The national cause was supreme so I stood up against the ways and hush-hush actions of Shri Joginder Singh for which I was jettisoned. To me this does not matter personally but what matters is that even despite specific complaint nothing could happen against the big people in this nation whatever authority may be approached. I wonder what line of action I should adopt. Whether it should be through the press or through the court if I want any action against any person in high places? I seek your kind guidance and help. I hope this time I will get some response from yourself personally as this is my 5th DO letter in the series in addition to the personal visits that I had paid in 1999 when I was still in Delhi.

Yours sincerely,

(B.R. Lall)

Shri N. Vittal,
Chief Vigilance Commissioner,
Central Vigilance Commission,
Starkta Bhawan,
Block 'A', G.P.O.,
I.N.A., New Delhi.

Appendix – VIII

565265 (R)
Tel. : 561838
Fax : 571629

D.O. No.3670

B.R.Lall,IPS

Director General of Police &
Chairman-cum-Managing Director
Haryana Police Housing Corporation Ltd.
211, Sector 6, Panchkula

Dated the 27.7.2001

Dear

You may kindly recall my meeting with you on 26th December 2000 which is last in the series after I complained against Shri Joginder Singh former Director CBI, vide may DO letter dated 1.1.99 which I followed with four reminders and this is sixth communication in the series. At the time I filed the complaint, you had just taken over and now you are completing your tenure, but the specific charges of bungling by Sh. Joginder Singh that I brought to your notice, remain unattended, though 31 long months have elapsed by now. Actually I had planned to raise these issues at the press club on 29.12.98 at the function for release of his book 'Inside CBI' but when I reached there and saw you in the Chair, I restrained myself, thinking that it may be construed as a reflection on CVC of the country who had just been appointed under the statute. Releasing book of a person against whom I was making such serious allegations, I thought, may embarrass you. This consideration weighed heavy with me, so I decided to retreat and instead raised the issues with you on 1.1.99, but all that I received after my persistence for two years, was an endorsement from Sh. Hardial Singh, Addl. Secretary to the Commission reminding Director CBI on 17.10.2000 and complete silence thereafter.

You have been advocating cultivating of values, cleansing the muck of corruption, and raising efficiency through electronic devices and otherwise, which perhaps had raised my expectations from you very high. In the process I forgot that in this country one should not go by rhetoric as everybody is either helpless at the time of action or not prepared for the unpleasant action particularly against the big wigs.

Since I have been concerned with the problem of fighting corruption since my childhood, I keep on analyzing the problem, the actions of various agencies including the governments, the CBI, the CVC, the Enforcement Directorate, the Income Tax Directorate, the Customs and also State Anticorruption agencies. It is unfortunate that no one takes enforcement measures and in particular the anticorruption measures to the logical end in a consistent and an impartial manner. Not only me, but also the country pinned hopes on your office, but last when I met you on 26th December 2000 I was crestfallen by your response "what can I do".

War against corruption has three aspects. Investigation or Enforcement is one of them and is the most prominent, but other two the prevention and the education are no less significant. There has been no visible difference in the first i.e. investigation aspect, ever after your taking over. There are no plans or strategies visible to public eye or even the professional eye and also there are no magnificent results indicating any change. Nor any revolutionary step is visible in that direction. It is true that there could be many obstacles in the way and also you are lacking in infrastructure as you require an investigation wing in your office, but such lament on 26th December that government were not supporting your organization and 'CBI was not caring for your directions' and that none was happy with you, are of no avail or of satisfaction to me and many others like me who might have lodged complaints with you. If you felt so handicapped, you could have considered in time, whether to continue or not. You would have jolted everybody and done a great service to this nation which amongst other things has been ravaged more and worst by this monster called corruption and it was your privilege or responsibility to fight this monster.

There is great scope in the field of prevention as also the education. That war could have been waged by your office itself by looking into the procedures and plugging the loopholes by making corruption difficult if not impossible. Also by enquiring into specific complaint of very serious nature by yourself or your office, would have had preventive effect. If CBI was not prepared to investigate or comment on its former boss, the files of the five cases that I had reported, could have been summoned in your office which I am sure CBI could not say no. Even otherwise, when a complaint is against the chief or the former chief of an agency; in all fairness, it should not be looked into by the same agency, but by another independent, preferably a superior agency, which in this case could be none else than the CVC. If action is taken on these issues and such other complaints, then only others in the government would refrain from indulging in such wild bunglings. It is in this context that to prevent bunglings in future, investigation into the complaints made by me is necessary.

In the field of prevention, ever since you took over as CVC, the only substantive step taken to my knowledge is, the issuing of the circular prohibiting post tender negotiations with parties except the lowest. This is a good step, but could there not be many more steps which could have made visible difference by plugging various loop holes.

With proper emphasis on prevention, coupled with proper action, I am sure scams like SEBI, UTI and many such others which have been occurring day in and day out for the last many decades, would have stopped. There is unlimited scope for stopping drain of wealth, from the country, which continues through overinvoicing/under invoicing of Imports/Exports and by inflated Project costs. The last in particular can be very effectively checked by exercising preventive options through agencies dealing with economic intelligence. Besides, some effective and potent steps could have been taken for unearthing the Disproportionate Assets which are burgeoning everywhere. This is necessary not only against Public Servants but also against business, industry and professionals through Income Tax Department etc. Preventive methods yield much more by prevention as it restraint bulk of offenders whereas investigation proceeds against the current subject only.

Similarly in the field of education, the masses could have been educated, how they are being cheated and how they should not get cheated, why they should help in catching the corrupt and how can they help in the process? Doordrashan could have been utilized for transmitting the message down the line upto the simplest villager to inculcate the confidence in him to ask for display of the records of the Panchayat, the BDO office and other government offices at the grass root level so as to ensure that funds meant for the lowest are not frittered away and reach him in full. This requires repeated telecast in the form of instructions, demonstrations, skits, serials, but nothing such has happened. The flood of corruption like all water flows downwards and drowns the lowest. There is need to strengthen the lowest so that he can keep his head above and can fight successfully the fury of these violent floods which are out to drown him completely. This has happened, as per their circumstances, in other countries who boast of having fought corruption successfully. But unfortunately not even a beginning has been made in our country. The institution of CVC under you could have educated the people.

There is another aspect to education. Students at schools, colleges and universities could have been sensitized so that we take care of the future generations and build resistance in them. The younger a person, the higher the potential for inculcation of values.

I have whole plans and schemes to fight corruption, but now stating them here is of no use as you are completing your tenure and earlier I did not want to state these as I was a complainant and I could have been misunderstood and accused of influencing you instead of pushing the merits of the case. I wonder if while leaving you can leave behind some legacy so that in future some effective steps could be taken by your successor. I close this letter with a pall of deep disappointment after offering to extend all help that was required and after pursuing it with no less a person than the mighty CVC. However, I am endorsing a copy of this letter to

Sh. V.S. Mathur, Vigilance Commissioner, so that something may be done in future.

Yours faithfully,

(B.R. Lall)

Sh.N. Vittal,IAS (Retd.)
Chief Vigilance Commissioner,
Satarakta Bhawan,
New Delhi.

Endst.No. 3671 dated Panchkula, the 27.7.2001

A copy along with a copy each of previous correspondence is forwarded to Sh.V.S.Mathur, IPS (Retd.) Vigilance Commissioner, Central Vigilance Commission, Satarakta Bhawan, Block A, GPO, INA, New Delhi for information and such action as may be deemed fit.

Director General of Police and
Chairman-cum-Managing Director
Haryana Police Housing Corn. Ltd.
Panchkula.

DA : 1. My D.O. Letter No. DIR(R&D)/1/Misc./99 dated 1.1.99
2. My D.O. Letter No. DIR(R&D)/1/Misc./99 dated 16.2.99
3. My D.O. Letter No. 5263 dated 22.8.2000 (with enclosures)
4. My D.O. Letter No. 5768 dated 22.9.2000
5. D.O. Letter No. 99/HMA/14 dated 17.10.2000 from Sh. Hardyal Singh , Addl. Secy., CVC to Sh. R.K. Raghvan, Director, CBI.
6. My D.O. Letter No. 6989/PS/CMD/HPHC dated 1.12.2000

Chapter – V

Lessons from Bhopal

Bhopal case has been a tragedy of errors, commissions and omissions that extended from non-appreciation of the situation, delays, pressures, disregard to the sufferings of the lay people and all that; where every wing of the state slipped and the judiciary had the steepest fall. Bhopal tragedy has also exposed our working styles and capacity to take on calamities. Things have certainly changed after the advent of National Disaster Management Authority that can take action to mitigate the effects, look after the people, their medication, rehabilitation, etc. However, the investigation and the trial part have neither improved nor received any attention. We have not looked into the efficiency and efficacy of police investigations, their will and infrastructure to act independently and their will and determination to measure upto the pressures. Further, we have also not looked into the trial processes of the judiciary. We have first to analyse their problems, procedures, calibre and their will to act and then analyse the causes of their failures. The answers to all the questions will just follow. As we have seen, the investigations took full three years, though it was not a task of more than 6 months. In the process the arrest of Anderson was messed up. The trial by judiciary should have been over by 1985 end or early 1986, but took decades and still the justice continues to be a mirage.

There were delays right from the beginning. First, even after four days of the event, the enormity and the seriousness of the situation were not appreciated. The same Section of law i.e. 304-A stood even at the time of arrest of Anderson and others. By 7th, the basic reasons that led to the leak should have been clear for not only the quick investigations, but also for taking the curative action to prevent the leakage any more. No doubt the police were busy in arrangements connected with looking after the injured and the dead and they could not do any thinking, but still the professionals should not have missed that at the time of arrest. Once the CBI took over the investigations, they also spent full three years in filing the chargesheet. It is, however, a different matter that the CBI did a clean professional job, collected evidence and obtained expert opinion from the distinguished scientists in details and filed the chargesheet under the appropriate much more serious an offence that was made out instead of sticking to the sections as recorded in the FIR. But three years is too long a period for investigations.

After filing of chargesheet in December 1987, the judiciary did nothing for full 14 months when in February 1989 an agreement was reached between Government of India and the Union Carbide that not only toned the demand of $3.3. billion to a mere sum of $470 million, but more serious is that criminal liability was thrown out. It took another two years to get the criminal liability restored and bring the case back on rails. Again the judge took two years for framing the charge that was challenged immediately in 1993 in the

High Court for non-existing issues. One wonders what was the stage for such an issue being raised and being entertained and deliberated upon by the High Court? Another two years were lost by the time the High Court passed the judgment, but the same was immediately challenged in the Supreme Court that again took one more year in giving its judgment. In toto another five valuable years were lost on this insignificant point without commencement of the trial in the case. Further the Supreme Court judgment diluted the offence and reduced it to a very ordinary one. Basically there was no occasion or even any reason earlier for the High Court and later for the Supreme Court to have entertained this issue at that stage as the Apex Court itself observed in great details in their own judgment in context of the High Court entertaining the same. They virtually concluded that perhaps the petition should not have been entertained u/s 482 of Criminal Procedure Code as the intervention of High Court was not required at that stage, which should actually be attracted only towards the rarest of the rare case. But having said so, they entertained the case themselves as well and toned down its severity, thereby almost finishing the case itself.

Quite a few questions arise that why at all it happened like that. The most serious part was the signing of 1989 agreement. As observed earlier if anything, the compensation should have been enhanced from $3.3 billion if the criminal liability was being dropped. The dropping of the criminal liability clouded every other step and the amount received was not adequate to fulfil all the monetary requirements of the people. How and why this agreement was entered, needs to be looked into and the responsibility at the governmental level for entering into such a detrimental agreement needs to be fixed and people held accountable and taken to task.

There had now been a view that appeal be filed in Session Court or the High Court. That both, in my view, were redundant and unproductive and would only have been further waste of time as has happened earlier in this case at every stage. The Supreme Court ruling reducing the gravity of the offence from 304 Part II to 304-A IPC still stands. No court other than the Supreme Court can restore it. The Government/CBI now have rightly filed the review petition directly in the Supreme Court for review of its judgment of 1996. It is heartening that now Government has decided to file curative petition in the Supreme Court, but it is sad that even this decision has taken another nearly six months.

An allied question is why the review petition was not filed in 1996. Details have been discussed earlier. Enough to add that now the responsibility needs to be fixed at all levels wherever there was a lapse in 1996. Since CBI files in this context will be very clear and helpful, there should be no problem in determining accountability on this score specifically. The Director, CBI of that time and the Personnel and Law Ministries have to explain. Besides CBI, the files of the ministries will also speak but only if the CBI had made a reference to them, otherwise it will be the sole responsibility of the CBI.

A great debate is raging regarding the nuclear liability bill. The cap as proposed was just Rs 500 crores which has been enhanced to Rs one thousand crores. We have seen how $470 million (Rs 2045 crores) fell terribly short. It is amply clear that the amount of $470 million was not adequate for Bhopal and the group of ministers have recommended for adding another amount of Rs 1500 crores making a total of almost $800 mn or Rs 3500 crores. With inflation, relief to that extent may now require something like $2 bn. As compared to any nuclear emergency (God forbid), all others including the Gas Tragedy of Bhopal appear to be the most ordinary. Even $2 bn may not be adequate. It is worth noting that as per report in *The Times of India* of

4th December, Government of India has filed a petition in the Supreme Court seeking an additional amount of Rs 7844 crores as compensation from UCIL, DOW Chemicals etc. who inherited the UCIL and the UCC. The amount claimed is on the basis of capitalization of the amount required in 1984, but at current prices it works out to above amount when the original amount of $470 m or 2045 crores is added, it gives Rs 10000 crores or $2.2 bn. As such, fixing any cap is not correct. We have also seen how liabilities have extended to billions of dollars in case of Oil Spill case of British Petroleum recently. There was no cap on that. Why should there be any cap in the case of India. This discrimination meted out to the third world needs be done away with. No one from outside will fight our cause. We have to take up our cause and fight our battle ourselves. The provisions should lay down certain criteria and scales. The extent of the total claim should depend upon the size of the tragedy and the extent of the damage, though, God may spare us from such eventuality, but when provision is being made, one has to visualize all the possible events threadbare. Not only the responsibility should be limited to any cap for the immediate sufferers but the responsibility should extend to at least 60 years as the effect of nuclear radiation passes down to generations after generations and we should take care of three generations at the minimum. Moreover, the stringent provisions will act as deterrent to any laxity as shown by UCC in Bhopal. If India were known for stringent laws and strict enforcement, UCC either would have changed the plant as they did in other places or would have closed it down long back. But since they knew they could get away easily, they paid no attention despite the fact that they were alerted a number of times.

- A number of lapses occurred as the investigating agencies work under the commands of the Government and not independently. As such the prejudices, preferences, compulsions and aberrations of all who matter keep creeping in and the final result quite often bears no semblance to the actual facts of the case. If state investigating agencies were not working under the pressure of the Chief Minister, they would have arrested Anderson at the appropriate time only, under appropriate sections of law and more important, would not have released him in a huff and much less escorted him like a VIP. They would have followed law and procedures. The agencies charged with collection of facts had to extend VIP treatment to a person charged with crime, lowering down their own morale, self-esteem and public image only because they or in other words the law is subordinate to the executive. Investigators represent law and interference in their work is interference with the law of the land that amounts to subversion of laws.

Similarly, if CBI were not under the command of the executive, it would not have been a party to waiving the criminal liability in 1989. Further, as the case was restored in 1991, it would have renewed its efforts immediately to get Anderson back and there would have been no occasion for the Central Government to issue the missive in question for not pursuing the extradition proceedings. Further, if the CBI were on its own there could be no question of not filing the review petition in the Supreme Court against its judgment in 1996.

Judicial procedures need be examined for the inordinate delays that have occurred at every step. As against the CBI investigating for three years, that also I don't justify, the various courts occupied the space spread over 23 years. It was possible and the citizen would have liked and appreciated if all the court processes were decided within 6 months to 1 year including appeals, etc. and then the court could have taken the CBI to task for spending three long years. Now court can have no moral authority to advise the CBI as performance of the CBI was far better as compared to the performance of courts right from the Lower Court of CJM to the highest, i.e. the Supreme Court. It is difficult to visualise how the courts can manage to spend and justify so much time. This and a few other cases require to be researched in details by some specialized research or academic organisation, so that procedures are amended and set forth to cut down all the delays. If such judicial delays are non-existent in most of the countries, why not in India. If we compare the burden of case work in India and abroad, we find that Indian judiciary is not so hard pressed as it is made out to be.

Besides delays, the courts also need to think over how much time to allot to usual objections and filing applications for delaying tactics that start in VIP cases from day one of the filing the FIR and extend till the trial concludes:

The moment a case is registered delaying tactics start for:

a) Quashing the FIR.

b) Staying the FIR.

c) Staying investigation

d) Putting in bail applications again and again.

e) Challenging jurisdiction of the Court

After completion of investigation the delaying tactics may be by way of:

1. Challenging the chargesheet.
2. Stay at any and every stage right from the beginning to the end of the case.
3. Frequent adjournments for various reasons of which most are unconvincing and are delaying tactics.

   Such like many more tricks are applied.

Obviously it is more so wherever big names are involved.

Even if the accused may fail at all the steps, he would have achieved his goal of delaying the proceedings, enjoying liberty and the fruit of crime. With the passage of time the accused makes out a case, as a sufferer, under Article 21 of the Constitution under which the provisions for quick justice to the accused are interpreted. A number of cases have been thrown out by the courts for being under trial for prolonged periods though the cases were pending in courts only and most of them were under stay for one lame reason or the other.

A major question being debated now is about bringing back Anderson. Though we should keep mounting the pressure on the US Government and various others concerned, as that may pressurize DOW Chemicals to enter into fresh negotiations. In any case efforts at his extradition would not be of much relevance and would hardly be fruitful for the simple reason that when he was released on bail, offence registered was under Section 304A which is a bailable one. Though he was arrested under Section 304 Part II IPC, but till the offence itself was shifted to that section, it is of no consequence. Also the Apex Court diluted the offence and at the moment no case exists under Section 304 Part II and no country will be willing to extradite its citizen for a minor offence like 304A IPC. He, no doubt, has committed further offence by absconding, but still it would be better that before we press, the Indian administration and the courts show a sense of urgency now at least and revise the offence to culpable homicide not amounting to murder. Secondly, though the Supreme Court order is silent about downgrading the offence to 304A IPC against Anderson specifically, but the rationale is simple that he was not a petitioner and the court decided the case of petitioners. Case of Anderson is similar to that of Keshub Mahindra and others and if 304 Part II does not stand against Keshub Mahindra, it will not stand against Anderson at all. Third, he is now 90 years of age and as such, it will be very difficult to fight out the case in US courts against Anderson at this age as everyone will be sympathetic to him rather than to our delayed pleas. Things would have been different 20 or even 15 years back. Further if compelled, Anderson is likely to feign loss of memory, or some other ailment that the VIPs normally resort to, or put up some other excuse so that courts in US could refuse his extradition.

DOW Chemicals that took over the Union Carbide refuses to own any responsibility as it argues that meeting the liabilities of the UCIL was not its responsibility as per the terms of Sale/Purchase. But it is common sense that only they have to shoulder all the responsibilities as one takes over a firm, it is both assets and liabilities that pass on simultaneously. Since DOW Chemicals is working in India in a big way, steps including blacklisting can be taken against them to break their callousness. Also whatever assets they own in India, could be impounded and confiscated if they continue to be recalcitrant.

Bhopal being a very big tragedy, no compensation can be adequate. People have lived through hell but no one can set the arm of the clock back. Toxic elements are still there not only on the ground and in the air, but the most serious is the toxicity in the atmosphere of the entire criminal justice system, the political system, that have filled the public life to dangerous proportions. It will be worthwhile if this occasion is used for cleansing the whole of Bhopal as also cleansing the public life for which the following fundamental steps in addition to the ones enumerated above are also suggested:

- Free all the investigating agencies from all sorts of influences and controls making them strictly accountable to multimember nonpolitical and non-bureaucratic bodies. If the courts require independence, the investigating agencies also require the same with much more intensity and urgency. If true facts are not brought before the courts they can't do justice and if investigation is not independent, true facts can never come before the court and justice will be the casualty as the court will only be groping in the grave-like darkness, in the words of the famous English poet William Wordsworth "In darkness lost, the darkness of the grave." This is the existing scenario of criminal justice system on the ground in all the big cases in particular and if the real justice ultimately happens in such a case, well it might be the rarest of the rare case. Though independence of judiciary is often talked and we are proud that the Indian judiciary is independent, but nobody talks of freedom of investigating agencies. During various discussions on Bhopal Gas Tragedy, the knowledgeable people, including those from legal fraternity, expressed their legalistic views that investigating officers are paid for collecting facts without being pressurised. That they are paid from the exchequer not to get pressurised. That if they fall to pressure, it is their weakness that they succumb to and should resign if they cannot measure up to the task. Well, if it is so simple, judges are also paid from the same exchequer and they are also supposed not to succumb to any pressure and do anything wrong, then why judiciary specially requires independence? Why have they been made independent or freed from the executive controls? After all the lower judiciary was separated from the executive in 1960s after realising this very problem. Why specially ensure freedom of Election Commission, the CAG and other constitutional functionaries as they are also paid from the same exchequer and are supposed not to yield to pressures. If police officers from SHO onwards are supposed to stand up on their own, why these big functionaries cannot shoulder all the pressures and stand on their own and require to tread on the crutches of independence. Incidentally all these constitutional functionaries are much above in the warrant of precedence and in status as compared to the senior most police officers in any State or even the Director of the CBI. If police at much lower levels right from SHO onwards are expected to function according to law despite pressures and ward them off successfully on their own, the same logic also applies to the judiciary and all others as well. Actually both the investigator and the judiciary equally require independence to function in a free and impartial manner more than any other denomination or any of the constitutional functionaries. The need for independence of the investigating agencies is much more than even the judiciary as it initially sets the ball rolling and judiciary deliberates on the basis of what the police present to them.

Judicial delays in Bhopal Gas case have been killing and this is a common denominator in all the cases handled by them. It is not the word of law that is so much deficient, but it is the implementation procedures that lead to the delays. Responsibility for everything that happens in the court is on the presiding judge. Basically judiciary has never self-introspected and the judicial procedures have never been studied, examined or researched and have remained static since the ages. I made a humble effort to study the same in CBI in 1995 and the results were eye opener. On judicial side the problems were with adjournments, bails and stays and nonappearance of accused and their lawyers, particularly the senior counsels. These findings were brought to the notice of the judge presiding over the exclusive CBI Court at Jabalpur, who readily agreed to implement law and procedures in letter and spirit in the enlightened manner. The disposal improved from an average of just 1.5 cases a year for the last 12 years to 46 cases for a single year by 2000, a whooping rise of 31 times or 3100%. A judge who has will and can enforce discipline can do wonders. It is possible to look into this aspect both from the record of the courts or from the court diaries maintained by the CBI in every case for every hearing in the court.

- There is a need for setting up a National Commission on Criminal Justice System to look into all these aspects. However, for making it useful there is a precondition that neither a judge nor anybody else from the legal profession should preside over this commission, as he is likely to start with a closed mindset as nobody can be a judge for his own actions or the actions of his own fraternity. At the same time the views of judiciary have to be taken into account and given due weightage and importance, respected and considered, so one of the members should be from the judiciary and another from the legal fraternity. Besides, one or preferably two of its members should be the eminent retired police officers as police are the biggest client of the judiciary as 70% of the cases in courts pertain to the criminal side. The commission must have representatives from the bar as well. The number of members from the legal profession should be less than half the total number of members on the commission.

- Besides the above lessons, there is another very important issue. Investigations have shown that the Gas Plant was suffering from many problems that were known to the staff working at the plant and to the senior officers. They cannot deny this knowledge as investigations have projected the same being communicated by UCIL to Union Carbide at Hong Kong and its headquarter in USA. It is for this reason that culpability of Anderson could be nailed and he could be chargesheeted. If this fact was not in his knowledge, he or Union Carbide could not have been chargesheeted. The Plant Manager and other officers could have played a crucial role when it was known that plant was defective and it was risky to run it. The Chairman of UCIL or some other officer down the line should have taken the initiative for closing down the plant. Somehow Indian managers are subdued when it comes to facing the bosses and in particular the foreign ones. If only some Indian had shown guts and concern for the fellow citizens and closed down the plant, the law would have been on his side. He could even have approached the police and the administration and got the factory closed in public interest under the orders of the appropriate authority as it was risky to run it but unfortunately we lack guts and do not muster courage to take such action. It is however a lesson for future not to look the other way round and face the problems straight. Fear is one thing that we have to cast aside.

BHOPAL GAS TRAGEDY OVER THE WEB

Two issues have very prominently been raised on the web by the US media regarding liability of Anderson as the CEO of the holding company and secondly liability of the UCC and Anderson after the compromise/agreement of 1989 approved by the Apex Court of India. Questions regarding personal liability of Anderson have been raised in certain sections of the media as also in the corporate world in India. With such a responsibility being passed on to the top corporate management they feel problems arising for themselves at sometime. It is argued on behalf of the CEOs and other senior functionaries that they do not know everything in details about all the plants and establishments that they command all over the country or all over the world as the MNCs have their operations worldwide. It may not necessarily be possible even in a single plant as they cannot be everywhere every time.

The most important issue that arises here is that they are the controllers of the show, they appoint the personnel, assign them the particular job, they lay down the policy how the establishment/business/factory or any other unit is to run. They only plan the blueprints and supervise their execution. They also plan the technical designs, the safety and security aspects. For the above or any other functions, finances are all in their hands. Plants and businesses are run under their close supervision. At the same time it is also correct that they cannot supervise the day-to-day functioning of every worker or officer. Under these circumstances there is merit that they cannot be held responsible for laxity or negligence of staff on day-to-day basis. If, however these issues are brought to their notice by their subordinates, the CEOs then have to be accountable and assume responsibility for every such issue. But they cannot wash off their hands off their primary responsibility in planning, in design, in not employing suitable hands or not spending on enforcing safety and security provisions. If problems regarding these fundamental issues are in their knowledge or if they were negligent in planning and/or execution, they and only they have to be held responsible. It would be advisable that the leaders in private sector evolve certain guidelines. The State as regulator should ensure that such regulations are enforced by the industry itself. But at the same time they have to own the responsibility or alternately they have to be held responsible and accountable under the law and duly punished for any criminal liability and penalised financially in their personal capacity as well. Under the law, this position obtains even now. The proverb "uneasy lies the head that wears the crown" fully applies to them and they are to be held more responsible and fully accountable subject to the analysis above.

Liability of Anderson and others in Hong Kong as also the top brass in India has to be determined on the above principles. He could be held responsible for any offence, only if he had personal knowledge that the plant as such suffered from various defects that were likely to lead to leakage and cause the consequential accident leading to the crime of culpable homicide. If on the other hand he had no such knowledge, it may not be possible to charge him for a rash and negligent act even.

It was a widely known fact right upto the top of UCC, including Anderson, that running Bhopal plant was fraught with risk. New designs and drawings had been sent to them from India as well. The risk of running a plant of existing design was known and it is for this reason that UCC had already introduced better designs at its plants all over the world except India. Actually UCC had already discarded as unsafe similar plants all over the world. It was in the knowledge of Anderson and it is with his consent and orders from the parent company that the plant at Bhopal had been put for sale and no further investment at its renovation or repair was sanctioned. Since it was within his knowledge as CEO/Chairman and under his directions that all new expenditures on this plant were on hold, he has to shoulder full and complete responsibility, more than anyone else. The question how far is the responsibility of a busy CEO, has been thrashed above and the shield of being busy can afford no protection against criminal liabilities once it has been established that it was in his personal knowledge. Incidentally a series of warnings had emanated from various sources from time to time. A list of the same appears as Appendix - IX to this Chapter.

In, USA it is also being argued on behalf of Anderson that if he were even remotely suspecting his arrest, he would have avoided coming to India, whereas he was so considerate that he came running to India on hearing about the tragedy. Before taking any view on the above, the condition at Bhopal as also the attendant circumstances will have to be seen. The city was under complete shock on 7th December, the day Anderson visited Bhopal. People were preoccupied with problems of their health and disposal of the countless dead bodies. They were still grappling with the unprecedented tragedy. Till then practically no investigations had been conducted and as such nothing had been visualised as to what had gone wrong. Nobody had any clue to what had caused that tragedy, so arrest of Anderson or for that matter of anyone in India was still not an issue amongst the people. There was no demand from the public to arrest him nor had people raised any such voice till then. Anderson from his sources in Bhopal and US Embassy in New Delhi must have ascertained that his arrest was not an issue till then. In that case why at all the need arose for Anderson to seek assurances in advance as the accounts have now turned out from the statements/accounts from so many sources including Rasgotra, Streeb and GK Reddy of *Hindu*. When in India no voice had been raised, then why did Anderson think on these lines and sought assurances in advance? Only much later it transpired during the investigations that the issues relating to defective design and the risks involved in running the plant as it is, were in his knowledge. This may not have been known to the world at large at that time, but Anderson himself knew it for sure. So naturally he must have been feeling guilty and apprehensive and as such took necessary precautions against the self-perceived exigency of his arrest. He travelled all the way to Bhopal only after obtaining due assurances.

Assurances could only have been extended by the Government of India as all talk on diplomatic channels is with them and not with the State Government. Perhaps the same was not conveyed down the line to the State Government, so the state took its own independent decision. By now Arjun Singh the then Chief Minister has admitted but linked it to disturbed conditions in Bhopal, which by itself is completely incorrect. In media also some mention has been made that the arrest was at the initiative of the State Chief Minister who probably saw it as an opportunity to win hearts of the people by prompt arrest of the management of the UCIL along with Anderson. Elections were only a few weeks away and this gesture could be converted into some votes at the hustings for which our politicians are too keen and would not like to miss any opportunity whatever be the occasion.

Here it is adequate to observe that by seeking assurances in advance, Anderson proved that he believed that he had done some wrong somewhere for which he was guilty and felt threatened on his own about his guilt.

The second issue is the perception that criminal liability of all the accused persons including Anderson has been settled once the comprehensive compromise was reached in 1989 that had not only the approval of the Government of India but also the seal of the Supreme Court. It has been brought out clearly that the Apex Court had only mediated between the parties to evolve a consensus at a middle figure of $470 million from the offer of $426 million and the then demand of $500 million. Supreme Court did not decide the quantum, but only bridged the gap in the otherwise out of court settlement. Damages could be negotiated, but not the criminal acts. There is no such provision in Indian legal system to abrogate the criminal liability. Even the Act of 1985 does not give any such power. This part of the deal was illegal, inhuman and ill-advised. A patent lapse can always be corrected despite perception to the contrary in the US and the Supreme Court corrected it in 1991. The order as it applies to Keshub Mahendra will automatically cover Anderson as well, as the two are exactly in the same position. There cannot be any doubt that the criminal case against Anderson also stood revived along with others in 1991.

The eternal lesson for us is that our diplomacy has to get stronger and aggressive rather than apologetic, meek, dumb and tame.

Appendix – IX

Previous Warnings and Accidents

A series of prior warnings and MIC-related accidents that were occurred:

- In 1976, the two trade unions reacted because of pollution within the plant.
- In 1981, a worker was splashed with phosgene. In panic he ripped off his mask, thus inhaling a large amount of phosgene gas; he died 72 hours later.
- In January 1982, there was a phosgene leak, when 24 workers were exposed and had to be admitted to hospital. None of the workers had been ordered to wear protective masks.
- In February 1982, an MIC leak affected 18 workers.
- In August 1982, a chemical engineer came into contact with liquid MIC, resulting in burns over 30 percent of his body.
- In September 1982, a Bhopal journalist, Raajkumar Keswani, started writing his prophetic warnings of a disaster in local weekly *'Rapat'*. Headlines, one after another 'Save, please save this city', 'Bhopal sitting at the top of a volcano' and 'if you don't understand, you will all be wiped out' were not paid any heed.
- In October 1982, there was a leak of MIC, methylcarbaryl chloride, chloroform and hydrochloric acid. In attempting to stop the leak, the MIC supervisor suffered intensive chemical burns and two other workers were severely exposed to the gases.
- During 1983 and 1984, leaks of the following substances regularly took place in the MIC plant: MIC,

chlorine, monomethylamine, phosgene, and carbon tetrachloride, sometimes in combination.

- Reports issued months before the incident by scientists within the Union Carbide corporation warned of the possibility of an accident almost identical to that which occurred in Bhopal. The reports were ignored and never reached senior staff.
- Union Carbide was warned by American experts who visited the plant after 1981 of the potential of a "runaway reaction" in the MIC storage tank; local Indian authorities warned the company of problems on several occasions from 1979 onwards. Again, these warnings were not heeded.

Chapter – VI

Conclusion

The narrative has established beyond doubt that all the decisions were taken at the highest levels in the Government of India as part of the expediency. Taking into account the administrative and the political culture of the country, no administrator would dare or even think of taking a decision like arresting or bailing out Anderson on his own. It also clearly brings out the strain of continuously running currents and undercurrents of pressures under which the governments and their departments function in our country as against the rule of law and well laid-out systems equitable for all. In handling of the Bhopal Gas Tragedy the pressures can palpably be felt right from the time of establishment of the factory at Bhopal in the seventies till 2010 when the judgment from CJM Court became public as also in its aftermath. If finally the group of ministers was constituted and it recommended various welfare measures including doling out Rs. 1500 crores and the same were all accepted immediately, even it was all because of the positive public pressure that the media debate exerted and focused on the Government. All these problems of the people had existed all through since 1984, but they suffered silently and helplessly. Even the judgment in the case was virtually announced by the Supreme Court in 1996 by downgrading the offence and thereby ensuring that everyone was allowed to go lightly and no one was punished for any serious offence. Nothing changed since then to have compelled the Government to act, except the present public outcry.

The Government abandoned its function of looking after the welfare of the victims, but recently it has been under pressure from all sides. Under these extreme pressures, the Government has now petitioned for an additional amount of Rs. 7844 crores as compensation as against 2035 crores of original compensation negotiated. It is good that now at last they are gunning for a realistic amount. They did not entertain any such request till such time the super pressure by way of public outcry was mounted. It is sad but true, unfortunately though.

I am not aware and nor have I gone into the circumstances of establishment of the factory, i.e. if there were any pressures at the time of setting it up at this particular location or not as certain quarters made out in the media. But it appears certain that the pressures and compulsions commenced immediately after its establishment and these have been quite visible. It was known that the factory dealt with the hazardous substances, so some area around the factory was to be barred from locating the residential colonies. The State Government was duty bound to see that no residential colonies were built around the factory for a distance of say at least 2 kilometers, but as a populist measure to win cheap popularity, unauthorised colonies were allowed to mushroom right up to the border of the factory presumably under political patronage. The unauthorized colonies were not only allowed to spring up but were even regularized.

Perhaps it was the pressure of getting votes for which our politicians cave in day-in and day-out saying goodbye to all the rules, regulations and the national interest or the long term social interest. The politician refuses to see beyond the immediate vote bank and strives only for that, keeping all other considerations at bay.

The chain of pressures continued after the tragedy. As is usual, the police investigations in such and other important cases are kept open so that the investigations can be given the desired direction as per instructions from above at the appropriate time. This is nothing but an inbuilt extralegal, but accepted system of pressure that has all-round sanctity from those who matter and from the people in power in particular. In this case there was also a limitation that because of the unusual, uncertain and peculiar conditions in Bhopal, the investigation could not have picked up immediately even if free hand were given, but the politics was played at the first available opportunity again under the vote bank syndrome when without even changing the sections of the law, the CM suddenly decided upon the premature arrest of Warren Anderson, Keshub Mahendra and others from the management of UCC India. Irrespective of the fact that the registered case continued to be under Section 304A IPC, the arrest was made under the offence of culpable homicide not amounting to murder, obviously to show how benevolent the Chief Minister was but when the superior pressure came from Delhi the CM changed his tracks within hours and not only released Anderson from captivity, but also conferred the rarest of the rare honour asking the SP and the DM to escort him to airport in a royal style. The CM did not stop at that and went further in honouring Anderson by offering his personal plane for his exclusive journey to Delhi where he was duly received and also met the highest dignitaries of the land. Had the action of the CM been merit based, he could hold to the same or at least request for reconsideration to his bosses at Delhi, but if he himself can throw away all the rules and the laws, his seniors can always do so, as they naturally have the supreme capacity to pressurise.

By now this is also clear that the Centre had been under pressure immediately after the tragedy and promised safe passage to Anderson before he left USA for India. He must have left USA on the morning of the 6th. So he negotiated his safe passage on 4th or 5th but certainly by 5th the Centre had promised him the safe passage as is stated or suggested by none else but PC Alexander himself, amongst others. It is not in public domain what could have been the pressures or the compulsions but what is obvious is that no enquiries from the State Government were made. The Centre was not aware of the factual position but yielded to the demand or the pressure from the US just in routine which perhaps is a matter of habit with us as a nation that we respect the will of the foreigners more than our national interest and if the former happens to be from the West, then there is no limit to our bending or crawling. However, the situation could have been covered up and would not have caused embarrassment and all the drama could have been avoided if only the decision of the Central Government had been conveyed to the State Government before Anderson landed in Bhopal.

Immediately after the tragedy, some Attorneys from the USA started visiting India from December 1984, took letters of authority from the victims at Bhopal and filed suits for damages and compensation in the US courts. The process continued through January and cases worth over $15 billion are reported to have piled up in the US courts. The Corporates and the Government in the USA were obviously alarmed. It can be safely inferred that it was under their pressure that the Government of India brought out an Ordinance on 29th February 1985 that no Indian will file such cases in the US courts and that Government of India alone will file all these suits in India only. Legally all the suits filed in the US stood withdrawn. So great was the hurry that the Government could not wait for the Parliament that was scheduled to meet in March. A month later, when the Parliament convened, the Ordinance was converted into an Act of the Parliament by March end. All these cases stood withdrawn and the Government filed a consolidated case for $3.3 billion for total damages. It is correct that the whole amount of $15 billion for which the lawyers had filed the cases, would not have been decreed by the US courts. Further it is also true that bulk of the money would have been retained by the US attorneys, but at the same time it is also correct that still a few billions would have been received from the USA by the Indian litigants. The fact is that more and more were filing suits in the US at that time, the claims would have mounted to at least $20 billion. Even if Indians received 25% of the claims that were filed, the amount received would have been of the order of $5 billion. The Government would not have taken such a retrograde step that too in such haste without extreme pressure from the USA.

The above chain of continuing pressures is further corroborated by the continuous subsequent pressure in the case being tried in the Indian courts. The UCC made an offer of $350 million with reference to December, 1984 that rose to $426 millions along with interest till 1989. Strangely the Government pressed for only a claim of $500 million in totality that was just 15% of its own original claim and would be much less when interest is added to that claim. The Supreme Court finding the difference quite narrow brought the parties to the middle figure of $470 million. Here it may be clarified that the role of the Supreme Court was that of the mediator as the reading of Supreme Court judgment makes it very clear that the Apex Court only moderated and did not decide the case on merits. Incidentally lots more people had died since 1985 when the claims were filed and there was every reason to revise the claims upwards. Without any reason or rationale, no Government should have agreed for such a scaling down of its own estimates and the claims. It is obvious that there was pressure from the US Government as also the Corporates.

At that time in 1989, it appears that basically the pressure to rush through was for dropping the criminal liability. On its own no Government in its senses will agree for such a step. Criminal liability in face of such massive deaths cannot be compromised for money that too for such a trivial and insignificant amount though basically any amount is inadequate as by 1989 it had been very well established in investigations that the UCC Headquarters in USA had the specific knowledge about the condition of the plant and the risks to which it was exposing the people around. The chargesheet filed by the CBI in December 1987 clearly brought out these facts along with reports and opinions from the experts from the CSIR and other esteemed institutions. That possibly rang the alarm bells in USA forcing a hurried compromise in which the criminal liability had to be dropped. This all could not have happened except under the US pressure whose nationals were the beneficiaries. The US is known to go to any extent in its national interest and to protect its citizens.

Incidentally such pressure has continued even now as the recent communication from a US functionary to

Montek Singh Ahluwalia, Deputy Chairman of Planning Commission, suggests. Ahluwalia sent an e-mail on 30th July 2010 to Michael B Froman, Deputy National Security Advisor of USA requesting "I wonder if I can enlist your help on a matter relating to India's borrowing from the World Bank.... You may remember I had mentioned this as an issue when we discussed the IBRD capital increase in G20. The matter is coming up in the IBRD Board Audit Committee on Monday on which the US is a member. The management wants a relaxation for India. Could you speak to the treasury to get the US ED on our side?" Montek Singh made it also clear that the UK was voting in our favour.

On the same day, Michael Froman writes back to Montek Singh Ahluwalia. "We are aware of this issue and we will look into it. While I've got you, we are hearing a lot of noise about the DOW Chemicals issue. I trust that you are monitoring it carefully. I am not familiar with all the details, but I think we want to avoid developments which put a chilling effect on our investment relationship."

Neither Montek Singh nor Froman is connected with the issue nor has it been raised by the former, but still an inbuilt warning is very clearly discernible and pressure is very obvious that do not touch DOW Chemicals. The reader can draw his own inference. Thanks to the "Times Now" TV channel that broke this news and brought both the mails to public domain exposing the continuing US pressure from all sides.

After 1991 the court battles had ensued but there was no visible effort or seriousness at expediting the matters. When ultimately in 1996 the criminal liability was diluted, no review petition was filed. This is a very unusual situation. Neither the CBI nor any Government worth its salt will let it go like that except by specific design, for whatever consideration or pressure. It can safely be presumed in view of earlier discussions that under no circumstances could it be a bona fide lapse. It was certainly carefully deliberated a decision. The same mindset and pressures that had compelled the MEA to send the communication to the CBI not to press the extradition case of Anderson, as referred to by this author, had continued and was part of the same sequel and the mindset that continued even later, all through.

The same mindset and logic also applies to the release of and permission for the sale of shares of UCC. It may be recalled that UCC held 50.9% of the shares of UCC India. After the tragedy, there was an embargo on transactions of the shares of UCC so as to prevent the sale and transfer of the factory, but the embargo was allowed to be vacated, enabling the UCC to sell the firm to DOW Chemicals. There was no reason except pressure for such an action till the final decision in the case now in 2010.

Unfortunately, all governance in India is pressure based and not merit based. Even the national interest could be relegated to a backseat under the pressures. If still, in some instance, the national interest is served or the merit is upheld, it is only incidental. In our weak system of governance we cannot ward off any pressures and much less if these happen to be exercised from abroad or are seen as attracting the votes. In a democracy if Rule of Law is not respected and followed, the governments will bow to all sorts of pressures. The rulers in turn pass on the same treatment to the ordinary people exercising the pressures on them. In the process, the rulers turn autocratic, oppressive, tyrants and despots for the natives. There is no escape from the fact that all aspects of our governance are dominated and plagued by above description of people who will muzzle all the unpalatable voices and listen only when they (the ordinary masses) acquire the capacity to hit back and pressurise. All efforts were mounted with this end in view by a number of ministers and ex-ministers to silence the little information that I or anyone else had disclosed. This tendency and behaviour has led to very serious consequences. Spread of Naxalism is the result of this two-fold phenomenon of despotic, tyrant and exploitative rule accompanied with mafia style silencing of any voice against such atrocities. No wonder that the districts affected by Naxalism are on rise rather fast. In 1990 their number was only 16 that has escalated to 230 now, an alarming state of affairs indeed. If not checked, we may be at the threshold of a civil war very shortly. It is high time the governments start governing according to law in the interest of society and nation rather than their personal or extraneous interests.

All independent institutions have been killed or silenced and subverted. If only these institutions were functional normally, they would not have allowed such a naked sell out as has happened in the case of Bhopal. This is not the way of progressive civilised world boasting of democracy. Their institutions enjoy freedom. We need to emulate them. To start with, free all the investigation and enforcement processes from the executive control. As is prevalent in the civilised world, these institutions should be left answerable to law through the courts and other legal watchdogs, so as to enable them to redeem their soul that these interest groups have snatched.

Further, it is most important for us to learn as a nation and particularly for the people in Government that there is no limit to yielding under pressure whatever may be the reason or rationale. But worst is to yield to pressures from abroad. In conducting foreign relations the only consideration has to be the self interest of our nation. We have to take lessons from Americans in particular. Froman is not concerned with DOW Chemicals and nor was the issue in question when Montek Singh wrote to him for getting help in raising a loan from the international institution, but he linked it with considering the case of DOW Chemicals. That may be a private firm but it belongs to the US. So without any connection he is looking after and defending the national interests of USA. As against that we obliged USA at every step to the extent of enforcing cruelties on our own nationals not at one point but on a number of occasions with the result that the gas victims are still suffering deprivations, privations, sickness, hunger and disease. The USA was quick to extract many pounds of flesh from the BP Oil leakages. If they, the richest country on earth, have no hesitation in doing so, why we compromised?

Same applies to the Nuclear Liability Bill. If we need nuclear power and want the deal to move further, they also have business interests, they are also interested in sale of their wares. We should negotiate the exigencies as per international norms. If we had not yielded to pressures and the international norms had been followed, we would not have settled for a poor half a billion but many billion dollars that was our due.

Index

Notes